Religious Ideas for Secular Universities

Religious Ideas for Secular Universities

C. John Sommerville

WILLIAM B. EERDMANS PUBLISHING COMPANY

GRAND RAPIDS, MICHIGAN / CAMBRIDGE, U.K.

Published 2009 by

Wm. B. Eerdmans Publishing Co.

2140 Oak Industrial Drive N.E., Grand Rapids, Michigan 49505 /

P.O. Box 163, Cambridge CB3 9PU U.K.

Printed in the United States of America

14 13 12 11 10 09   7 6 5 4 3 2 1

Library of Congress Cataloging-in-Publication Data

Sommerville, C. John (Charles John), 1938-

Religious ideas for secular universities / C. John Sommerville.

p.   cm.

ISBN 978-0-8028-6442-0 (pbk.: alk. paper)

1. Universities and colleges — United States — Religion.

2. Church and education — United States.

3. Secularism — United States.   I. Title.

LC383.S67   2009

379.2′8 — dc22

2009026542

www.eerdmans.com

For Tim, Penny
Mary Lyn, Jim, and David

Contents

vii

CONTENTS

IV. The University and the Culture Wars

Preface

T HE POINT of these essays is to expand the invitation I recently made to the academy, to engage in dialogue with religious colleagues where they were similarly wrestling with our most intractable questions. In that earlier book, *The Decline of the Secular University* (Oxford, 2006), I argued that the secular research university was having trouble thinking coherently about many of our pressing problems, especially concerning human distinctiveness and the human good. One of the main reasons for this, it seemed, is that a century ago universities became wary of considering ostensibly religious viewpoints on their merits. They did not anticipate that the current rationalism would come up short of answers to our practical concerns and leave so many arguments suspended. So my point was that America's universities could regain some of the social, cultural, and even political leadership that they may have forfeited by narrowing their perspective to rationalism and naturalism.

Universities now have a different purpose than they had in the 1890s, say, when secular research universities were launched. Whereas they used to be devoted to the discovery of reality, they are now largely about applying the knowledge we have. That, of course, means professional education, which some think of as the end of the university ideal. But it need not be. All professional education, without exception, serves some aspect of the human good, and ought to include serious reflection on human needs. This gives a new urgency to the very questions that religions have always addressed. But it comes at a time when science and even the "humanities" have been ignoring the very concept of the human. It is becoming apparent that the various attempts to deconstruct, scientifically "reduce," or relativize ideas of the human difference are revealing their absurdity. Serious reflection on the human is going to raise questions of ultimacy, which are religious by their nature.

Given its professional aspects, education today is likely to leave one alone at the point of decision, where one must decide how to apply our knowledge. So universities today are about choices as much as answers. One can go further, to say that they are not so much about proofs as about faith — understood as one's basic personal and intellectual orientation.

The numerous recent attacks on religion as *explanation* miss the main point, which is that religion is primarily one's *orientation.* Before you even embark on any line of argument about life, you have already decided the perspective from which you will proceed. Is the universe impersonal — and are you yourself included in that judgment, since you are part of the universe? Or do our intuitions of personality and values tell us something different about the universe, of which we form such an interesting part?

Whatever else religion is, it is how we make choices. The rationalism and naturalism in an educational system increasingly oriented toward professionalism are about how we inform our choices, but not about how we make them. The university's job should not be to tell us what choices to make, but it could do better at investigating the range of choices before us. That is, universities need to be conscious of religion. This of course involves becoming more conscious of the *differences* between religions, as delicate as conversations on the topic may be in a pluralistic world striving for tolerance.

For their part, religious voices need to consider what their contribution to academic debates might involve, beyond preserving the history and teachings of their particular heritage. We don't need more studies of religions so much as we need to detect the religious thinking within all of modern thinking. We need to see how quickly academic questions spill over into the realm of ultimacy, since, according to Paul Tillich's useful definition, our ultimate concerns amount to our religion. For example, we might show how science itself is a religious enterprise — the desire to comprehend our cosmos, inspired by the search for something like a mind behind it. Certainly, the belief that there is a practical point to such study brings science into the universe's "personal" realm.

All this comes at a time when it is easy to think that universities are hardly worth worrying over, since they have settled into such a humble job-preparation role. In the competition to shape our society's thinking, they are being superseded by the media and the Internet. That is a sad thought, since the deficiencies of the latter are all too apparent. Whether one is more secular or more religious, we all have an interest in bolstering the one institution that can offer a thorough airing of ideas and arguments, an enterprise that aims at wisdom as well as skills. For example, it is worrisome that government seems to want universities to be self-supporting, assuming they are merely an adjunct to the economy. Universities might be able to resist this pressure if they can show that they are more than that.

We need not think there are two sides — religious and secular — locked in conflict. We all stand to learn from a joint exploration of our concerns. More secular and more religious voices should be arguing toward discovery, more than toward victory. We can now see how naturalism, the default basis of our crumbling ideologies, is a nihilistic threat to us all, to the very idea of a human difference. Perhaps we will find that we can cooperate in pragmatic appeals to what we cannot deny (personality, for example) and what we cannot *not* know (justice, for example). One need not give these things some physicalist interpretation, as naturalism would attempt, but simply recognize that they are foundational to the very concept of higher education. By now we must all be tired of hearing that our choices are merely personal, political, or absurd. After all, nobody believes that — nobody who is trying to be part of the solution rather than part of the problem.

Each of the following chapters show how religious and even Christian views can make sense to a secular mind. They may, in fact, make better sense than many of the available alternatives. Some of the points will seem so ordinary that we may need to be reminded that they are in fact religious. My hope is that this will encourage those on all sides to explore their agreements as much as their differences.

A number of these pieces began as talks at the Christian Study Center of Gainesville, Florida, which was founded recently as an educational enterprise, attempting to dialogue with, rather than confront, the large, secular, public university across the street. Nothing wrong with confrontation, but it's not my gift. My thanks to the director, Dr. Richard Horner, and those colleagues, students, and townspeople who have made that such a vibrant place.

PART I

The Crisis of the Secular University

CHAPTER 1

Secularist Education Becomes Problematic

T HERE ARE several books circulating these days about how universities are failing. I wrote one too, and should begin by giving a sense of that book, for we will want to go beyond it to meet some of the questions it has raised.[1] Other critics of the university try to be practical, suggesting what could be done to restore the ideal. My book suggested something more drastic, maybe even a new paradigm in thinking about universities.

When I retired from university teaching, I could look back over fifty years as student or professor in a number of large, secular, private or state universities. That is nearly half of the whole history of what we call secular research universities, which only began in the last decades of the nineteenth century. I felt reasonably at home in them over the years, which may have kept me from being too reflective. But now that I was on the outside I was struck by how much had changed in that time. Of course universities are much bigger now than they were in 1956, when I was a freshman. They command tremendous resources, and produce more and more of whatever they produce. But still, it seemed to me that they had lost a lot in the meantime.

I don't think this was just me becoming jaded about an institution that I thought should be more special. I thought I was finally able to see our universities the way American society does, as a good way of prepar-

---

1. C. John Sommerville, *The Decline of the Secular University* (New York: Oxford University Press, 2006).

ing us for our jobs, but not where we look for answers to our important questions. There seems to have been a loss of focus as the institutions have sprawled, a loss of coherence as they have a harder time articulating what they stand for, a loss of confidence and prestige as they find American society going its own way.

As I remarked in the previous book, the most notable failure of our current universities is not teaching students how to *spend* their money. Amid all the programs that tell them how to make money and be useful, there don't seem to be any that discuss what is valuable in and of itself. Money, after all, is not an end in itself, but only a means to real ends. Are values only there to be "deconstructed," or to be explored? What might stand as our ultimate value? Is the university going to help students discover that? If not, you can understand why they don't look back after they graduate. I'm going to argue that this is where the secular university could use some help from religious sources. But first I want to go back to how things have changed in the last half-century.

As I remember things, it seems to me that the high point of the importance, or the sense of importance, of universities must have been around 1960. I was younger then, and more easily impressed, of course. But universities took it for granted that the whole world was undergoing Modernization in its institutions, and that universities would be guiding much of this development. The West seemed clearly the model in politics, economics, science, technology, law. Other areas of the world would surely follow our lead. Of course, this would involve a continuing secularization of cultures. This didn't necessarily mean religion would disappear, but it would become an entirely private matter, and could be ignored in our public debates and decisions.

What would replace religion, many academics supposed, would be something like rationalism. Rationalism is the sense that our "reason" is self-sufficient, self-validating. In relation to culture generally, we called this Modernism. We can think of Modernism as a sort of cultural Darwinism, being entirely open to change in art, music, literature, values, ethics, mores. We didn't need to protect traditions, as we'd worked so hard to do earlier. We would follow reason and nature into the heart of the human experience, under the guidance of our most creative spirits. That, in short, was Modernism in culture.

In the 1950s it was assumed that universities would play a central role in bringing Modernization to institutions and Modernism to culture. Of course, in those days we had to worry about the regimes in the Soviet Union and China, with their records of appalling inhumanity. So we recognized that we had to maintain the core values which would prevent the excessive materialism we saw over there.

In 1960 President Kennedy ratified this sense of the university's importance when he called on so many university faculty to staff his administration. This hadn't been done before; it hasn't been done since. To commemorate that triumph of the academy, the historian Richard Hofstadter published his *Anti-Intellectualism in American Life,* which put the university's critics in their place.

But you know what's coming next. The mid-1960s saw an explosion — not in Cuba, but in Professor Hofstadter's own Columbia University, and in universities large and small. Modernization and Modernism imploded, without outside intervention. Of course the student rebels were anti-war, but they were also anti-university. This was not a rejection of the tattered remains of our religious traditions but of the very Modernism that the university was helping to promote. Their complaint was that America was forcing these on the rest of the world. Our professions of democracy and internationalism were interpreted as imperialist. Who on earth would want to emulate America's record on race or poverty, or our aggressiveness abroad? So the 1960s saw a comprehensive attack on an Americanism that was already essentially secular.

By the 1970s faculties were joining their students' protests. Feminism, multiculturalism, and a relativizing history of science all helped to keep the shaking going on. In the 1980s the so-called postmodernists were making Modernism stand in the pillory, with a sign around its neck reading "Dead White European Male." Postmodernists succeeded in popularizing what philosophers had long known, that Rationalism is not self-sufficient. There are no self-validating rational principles at the basis of all thought. Thinking goes down to commitments that might as well be called faith. Or as they said, it is all political. Postmodernism was the more troubling for having come from inside the university. It didn't stem from McCarthyites or Moral Majoritarians or any of the other old enemies. Rather, it was reason's revenge on rationalism.

Nowadays, there is a new criticism of the university that focuses on its corporate organization and operation. This is not a big concern of the general public. Most of the public will support anything that promises to keep costs down and speed up the assembly line — and that, after all, is what the corporatization of education is about. But corporatization is a huge issue with academics. They see a whole way of thinking and learning being threatened. It seems that sometime in the 1980s, accountancy became the queen of the sciences. Universities are about money in a whole new way. They are now measured in terms of money — the size of their endowments, how much they can charge for tuition, and the return on that investment in the starting salaries of their graduates.

We have gotten used to calling the academy the marketplace of ideas. Markets are where money rules.

You can see that money has moved all the way up to the top of our scale of values. It trumps all other values, so that it doesn't have to justify itself. We can never have enough of it, because it is mistaken for an end in itself rather than as a means toward real ends.

When you think about it, the triumph of money is the final stage of secularization, if secularization means the separation of all areas of life and thought from religious direction. In the process of secularizing, it has become clear that all human values are connected in some way with religion, and we are strangely uneasy with that. Don't mistake me: markets are a blessing when furthering humane values. When they are allowed to become absolute rulers, markets can be monstrous. We will look at this more in the next chapter.

Market *freedom* is one value among many; market *absolutism* wipes out other values. So even secularist universities, like the rest of the economy, may be falling into the grip of an absolute. Surely we should reserve ultimate allegiance for something that takes the personal dimension into account, as money does not. Any absolute or final goal or concept should personalize our values, as religious concepts do.

How would one prove that the universe contains the personal? The very existence of universities should be proof enough, being a monument to the goals and purposes of humans. The universe itself is personal in the sense that it contains and nurtures persons, who appreciate knowledge and even truth, who value service, have purposes, and whose loves transcend mere desire. We haven't just blundered in from another dimension, but are as real in all our values, purposes, and loves as gravity or galaxies are real. Creation didn't end with the Big Bang, if we may think of ourselves as in the Creator's image in the project of creating universities.

When Richard Dawkins famously wrote, "The universe we observe has precisely the properties we should expect if there is, at bottom, no

design, no purpose, no evil and no good, nothing but blind, pitiless indifference," one has to wonder whether he ever looked in a mirror.[2] Where
did all those concepts come from, if not "the universe" — which, after all,
includes Dawkins himself?

Dawkins might answer that we only think we have a personality that
transcends our hydrocarbon structure because neuroscience is still
young. So we just need faith (!) until "we" can come up with a physicalist
reduction of consciousness. But who is this "we"? Of course he means
scientists, who show all the purposes, values, and even good intentions
that he effectively denies. Does he think all these personal qualities and
values stand outside "the universe" somehow?

Suffice it to say that universities don't make sense outside some
framework of humane values. Truth, service, academic freedom, and respectful debate mark universities off from more unaccountable think-
tanks. So it is troubling to think that the neglect of values other than
money is overtaking our universities.

This brings our history up to date. It only remains to note that despite the pounding that universities have taken, and the nihilism of a
corporatized education, universities have always been confident of one
area of continuing superiority: they could still stand aloof from the religious voices clamoring around them. The secular identity of the university is asserted perhaps more vigorously precisely because of the insecu-
rity of the rest of the Modernist project. The university's secularism used
to be taken for granted, but now America's religious populism has begun
to make academics defensive and even combative.

Surely this is one factor in the recent unprecedented attacks on religion as such, which would not have been thought necessary in the days
of a more confident secularism. They appear to be addressed to those
who had a university experience without being converted away from religion in the process. Whether the hyper-literal readings of religious texts
and unimaginative understandings of religious thinking in these attacks
convince those readers — or their authors — will reveal itself in time.

Before the 1980s, religion was rarely heard from around universities.
In 1951 William F. Buckley Jr. published *God and Man at Yale,* but it had
puzzled the academy more than impressed it. But by the 1980s, in the

---

2. Richard Dawkins, *River Out of Eden: A Darwinian View of Life* (London: Phoenix,
1996), 155.

wake of the resurgence of religion in world and American politics, historians were beginning to recount the *story* of the secularization of the university. In other words, they were able to problematize this secularization — to make it seem strange, rather than inevitable. George Marsden, Edward Purcell Jr., Julie Reuben, James Turner, and others were able to question where the secularization of education was taking us.

Sometimes, their story sounds more like a lament than a challenge. They wonder why universities are no longer the repositories of centuries of discovery, of human wisdom and creativity. It is hard even for them not to take the secular character of universities for granted. But as the new millennium dawned, I thought the time was right for a more basic challenge. It was time to point out not just what the university's secularity has done to society or to religion, but what secularity has done to the university itself, as it increasingly sinks into irrelevance.

*   *   *

What do I mean by irrelevance?

Most notably, universities are obviously not giving society any leadership. Take public opinion. It is striking how seldom we see professors on television. We could measure the importance of academics against all others by comparing the audience for C-Span or PBS, where you may see them, with the audience for all the rest of the networks and cable channels combined, where you will not. Out there in our virtual world, where we look for public opinion, you will rarely hear from an academic.

Or take politics. Would we ever have close elections if the universities were giving us political leadership? Given the self-report of our liberal-leaning faculties, the other side wouldn't even be able to keep things close. Or take culture. A commercialized pop culture seems to have totally eclipsed the more sophisticated culture that universities used to enshrine. The university's commitment to elective choice ensures that younger generations need not be bothered with any of the world's heritage of high culture.

Or take science. Scientists commonly lament that they must take their orders, along with their funding, from business and government. They aren't being asked whether they think NASA's budget could be better used elsewhere. Administrators at my university are proud to announce that we are now seventh in the number of patents awarded. So universities serve, but they do not lead. It's good to serve, but this lack of leadership is not what the founders imagined long ago, and it doesn't match the academy's sense of itself.

What do universities offer? Obviously, professional training. In my university, sixty percent of undergraduates take their degrees in professional majors. Eighty percent of graduate degrees are from professional schools. We've given students the power to make this change in our universities, as they follow the money. When I hear university presidents give speeches now, their worry is often whether other institutions will take over job training, or do it more quickly or cheaply. They are unlikely to mention developing our inherited wisdom to meet new concerns.

*   *   *

Here is where I may go against your expectations. I don't think professional training is unworthy of universities. It seems a perfectly natural development at this point, for I think a new paradigm of the university is emerging. In the first half-century of the secular university, the excitement was quite properly about the *discovery* of reality. But at some point along the way, the balance shifted to *applying* our knowledge. Nothing wrong in this; it is the justification for such large and expensive institutions. But we need to recognize that applying our knowledge always means applying it *for human benefit*.

How aware are our professional schools of that aspect of their job? What would they say was their goal? Helping the economy helps people. But how do we measure the help we offer? In money terms? Nowadays, that seems easier to argue than espousing some measure of the human good. The academy says that what one does with the money is a personal, or a political, decision. This amounts to an abandonment of a leadership role in American society. But where would professional schools look for help toward a deeper understanding of the human good?

What is the university's official understanding of the human good? Granted, it is an enormously complicated subject. Our initial reaction is to protest that people may differ. As a result, we see the university dismissing or actually undermining the concept of the human.

Take science. The sciences are charged with trying to find naturalistic explanations for as much of our behavior as possible. Naturalism seeks to use the terms derived from a study of the most basic elements we can analyze. Seeing how far such naturalism will take us is justified and leads to useful applications in medicine, psychology, and other fields. But there is always going to be a contested frontier between the natural and the personal, where naturalism seems to be invading another realm. You may be able to remember the heyday of "behaviorism," in which one did not look for the *meaning* of our actions, or even take that concept seriously. Or the efforts in the 1980s to colonize all human values within the terms of sociobiology. Evolutionary psychologists tried to reduce all values to survival value, thus denying any human distinctiveness. Our species, like the others, would be defined in terms of instinctual behavior rather than purposeful action, and we could rub out the line between humans and the rest of nature. When the results did not live up to promises, philosophical naturalists counseled us to wait until they could.

The frontier has now shifted to neuroscience, where journalistic reports suggest that being able to trace or measure the energies involved in mental activity will say all there is to say about our minds and spirits. Again scientists seem to be writing promissory notes on an overdrawn naturalism. After all, they would not agree that tracing the neural paths of *scientific* thinking would "explain" their science. Neural impulses would never account for the neuroscientists' intentions.

Oddly enough, when we turn to the humanities, we find a similar effort to dismiss the concept of the human. One would expect them to be defining the human in terms of its difference, as definitions try to do. But in fact they have recently been "deconstructing" the very concept of the human and the various human values. Portraying them as relative to different cultures and discourses leads to the notion that they aren't as real as the things philosophy or science deals in. It's not surprising, then, that some of those in the humanities would like to change that name to "cultural studies."

We can well believe that our understandings of "the human" are culturally contingent, and mostly a Western notion. But as Harold Bloom, the famous literary scholar, points out, this doesn't dispose of it. He enjoys flaunting a "Western" understanding of the human in the face of those critics whom he accuses of "occupying" his country.[3]

3. Harold Bloom, *The Western Canon: The Books and School of the Ages* (New York: Riverhead, 1994), 15-39.

When you think about it, science itself is a culture. Sciences are languages, useful for embodying the state of our knowledge. The linguistic turn in philosophy suggests that languages are as close as we can get to whatever-there-is. So one can easily see that science's very existence is proof that humans transcend their biological substance. The existence of the scientific project shows the scientists' superiority to what they investigate, just as the truths they aim for, transcend whatever neural impulses carry them. Likewise, the *uses* we make of the scientists' knowledge will not be dictated simply by our basic hydrocarbon makeup.

With all this confusion over what is real, we can't see how to move on to the vital question of human needs and the human good. Without renewed attention to this, our professional education is simply job training, and the very term "university" becomes obsolete. So it is unfortunate that these attacks on concepts of the human have come at just the time when the university has become so largely about professional education.

A new paradigm for the university could change things. Most especially, it would allow for a different relationship between science and religion. Back when the university's task was discovering reality, the burden was on religion to show that it had anything to offer. Now that the job is showing how to apply our knowledge, the burden is on science to show that it can make our choices for us. Religion has traditionally offered us the language we use for discussing the human and human needs.

*   *   *

Where do we go from here? If the university can only regain a position of importance by wrestling with concepts of the human, we will find that our concepts of the human were born in religious discourse and may be most at home there. It is commonly supposed that one can avoid a religious basis for discussing the human by alluding to Greek or Roman thought, as if such subjects can be grounded in "philosophy," pure and simple. What we forget is that the Greeks and Romans were religious, and their ethical notions reflect that. It would take a historian of philosophy to assess this case more fully, but when Plato cannot ignore the question of the "ends" of life, and when Aristotle cannot begin the *Nicomachean Ethics* without mentioning God (in the singular) as ultimate end, we see notions of purpose and ultimacy birthing Western philosophy. Certainly St. Augustine is a central figure in Charles Taylor's classic *Sources of the Self* for Augustine's importance for the emergence of "self," a major sense of the human at present.[4] In literature, Harold Bloom contrasts the primitive Homeric heroes, who are mostly "battle-grounds where contending forces collide," with Hamlet, "who is in the Biblical tradition of a human spirit."[5] Must such concepts be abandoned rather than developed?

Reviews of my previous book have noted that it is lacking in practical suggestions on what religion could now offer. This was partly by design, as I wanted to encourage others to engage in what might be a large venture. I didn't want critics to think that disposing of my few suggestions could end our thinking on the matter. We may need a fresh language to build a bridge all the way from theology to philosophy and on to professional preparation. But I can add a little here to the subject of what I think religious arguments would look like.

In general, of course, religious arguments will contrast with naturalistic arguments. They will be along the lines of personalist philosophies. Personalism is seldom known by that name, but it shows up in various philosophical traditions. As I use the term, personalism takes personal categories such as responsibility, justice, sanity, guilt, science, freedom, purpose, and truth as basic to understanding what we call the universe. Personalists wouldn't worry about anchoring these personal categories in physicalist concepts. As they see it, the most real things in the universe are those things that can act.[6] Action, as opposed to mere behavior, implies freedom and purpose. Whatever our objections might be to this approach, all of our intuitions indicate that persons do exist in the universe — as irreducibly as electrons or space. It seems to follow that we must begin certain discussions with the appropriate personalist terms, overcoming the Modernist physicalist prejudice.

So religious arguments will concern things like what is good in itself,

---

4. Charles Taylor, *Sources of the Self: The Making of the Modern Identity* (Cambridge, Mass.: Harvard University Press, 1989).

5. Bloom, *Western Canon*, 195.

6. Alan J. Torrance, "What Is a Person?" in *From Cells to Souls — and Beyond: Changing Portraits of Human Nature*, ed. Malcolm Jeeves (Grand Rapids: William B. Eerdmans, 2004), 199-222; John Macmurray, *Persons in Relation* (London: Humanities, 1991, orig. 1961); John Habgood, *Being a Person: Where Faith and Science Meet* (London: Hodder and Stoughton, 1998).

as against what is good as a means. They may concern what is ideal for human life, and take up questions of human rights in a more coherent way. They are likely to deal with our responsibilities to creation and to future generations. All of these concerns seem to touch on notions of ultimacy, of our final term and final obligation — again evoking Paul Tillich's definition of religion as one's "ultimate concern." What is worth dying for? How much inequality should we tolerate? What are the marks of a good society? Right now, the university is likely to declare these to be, again, either individual or political. But this shows the limits of a secular discourse that was adopted provisionally for the earlier purposes of discovery.

What I'm calling personalism has a natural affinity with religion. You would think it was also basic to what is called humanism. Historically, humanism gravitated toward naturalism and rationalism, to achieve an independence from religion. But it seems that humanism and religion may no longer be rivals so much as co-belligerents against the "vulgar naturalism" that trumps so many arguments in the secular university.

The human is what the new paradigm of the university should be about. And I would assert that "human" is best seen as a religious category. Attention to these points would give the public a stake and an interest in university debates, since the public seems more broad-minded than academics on these subjects. It might also give politicians a new appreciation for universities.

But what sense does it make to say that "human" is a religious term? It depends. If you want to describe the physiology and instinctual behavior of *Homo sapiens,* the outside of the subject, then you should use naturalistic terms. But if you want to describe human freedom and purposive action, the inside of the subject, you will need terms that are at home in a personalist, and ultimately a religious, discourse. They are religious in that they inevitably raise questions of ultimacy. While it is indeed necessary to see how far a methodological naturalism can take us, the ideology of philosophical naturalism needs to be questioned constantly. We should be warned that "human" and "humane" will turn out to have ethical aspects, as when we say that one person is more humane than another, or that another is "inhuman."

I am not saying that religious arguments should be entertained in the university just because they are religious. We shouldn't privilege religious arguments any more than we should privilege secular arguments just because they are secular. Initially, they've all got to strike us as plausible and helpful, as intuitively justified. Then we can find whether they make better sense of our situation than alternatives.

*   *   *

So my big point is that the university needs to consider religious voices, not just for their historical interest, but for the help we might gain from them. You may wonder whether this is directly against the constitution of the secular university. Was the founders' point in secularizing universities to open them to non-religious viewpoints, or to impose a non-religious viewpoint and single vision? Some of the historians I mentioned earlier make secularization seem rather accidental, especially as individual faculty members made an issue of their difference and courts assured them of a right to ignore their colleges' founding religious orientations.

It is difficult to guess where courts might go with these questions. When the Supreme Court ruled in 1963 that grade schools could teach about religion, but could not simply teach religion, they understood that this made religion of only historical interest, part of "a secular plan of education" as they put it. Back then the justices did not imagine that secular approaches might come up short, or that religion could actually help with some of our debates. Might they now decide that imposing a secularist ideology is as illegitimate as establishing a religion? In general, the Supreme Court has been less stringent in its demands of secularity in public higher education than in elementary schools or high schools. Might they realize that secularism is not rationality itself, but only a stage in the history of thought?

But is the reinsertion of religion really a pressing need? Aren't we muddling through reasonably well as things are? We need to think how many questions are on hold in American society that concern the logic of the human. As I listed them in the earlier book:

> What is a life worth, in terms of liability costs or tort settlements? Or in terms of victim restitution, wartime casualty counts, capital punishment? Beyond this, our vague ideas of the human underlie disagreements on sex education, city planning, human rights, poverty programs, biomedical hybrids, criminal punishment, art

galleries, public relations, health administration, general education requirements, conservation, to name a few.[7]

The list should go on, to prisoner interrogation, spanking, policies regarding fertility and mortality. I have a bad feeling that college classes
may raise these questions in an offhand manner — on the way to declaring them beyond the university's mandate.

Think how far short secular reasons come of concluding such issues.
Consider the topic of genetic enhancement of a fetus. Religions might
have different positions on the subject, and might be able to ground
them. Is there a secular position? Is there a secular position on who
should make the decision — whether parent, doctor, insurance company, scientific authority, government official, or elected politician? Our
power over children focuses many such questions. My mind goes back to
a course I taught on the history of the concept of childhood, where I offered my students a list of our dilemmas. Do we mostly want the child to
achieve, or to be happy? Should we try to make the child feel normal, or
special? Should we have a longer school day or year, or shorter, and why?
Should the state or the family be the final authority over the child, or
how should they divide the job? Should we treat girls and boys the same,
or differently, or would it depend? Is tolerance to encourage differences,
or to overcome them? Before the students' first glib answers had died on
their lips, they had begun to realize why our society is confused.

We don't know whether we should be arguing from what is good for
the existing society, or for the child, or for the adult the child will become,
or for the family that is the child's whole world, or for the society we want
to create. We don't know how long a time frame, how many generations,
we should be dealing with. We don't know how to justify our responsibility or authority over other humans. We don't know how to measure their
progress toward full humanity. And we would be hard pressed to say
which of our arguments were properly secular, or what made them so.

Even if religions offered answers, whether they were *religious answers* might be a question. We are all sort of amphibious in this regard,
not too conscious of our footing in our arguments. But I expect that
more satisfying answers might emerge from debate that allows religious
insights. I realize that it will be a while before religious arguments will be

7. Sommerville, *Decline of the Secular University*, 34.

forthcoming. Religious intellectualism has been kept alive in seminaries and religious colleges, but how much are these schools addressing our common questions? Having long been discouraged from participating in broader academic life, religions may need to be reawakened to their intellectual resources.

I will offer one suggestion about the structure of religious arguments in a more open university. Ordinarily it is assumed that religious arguments will start from first principles. This means confrontations between religious and secular worldviews. Religious worldviews may be well developed already, but are likely to be expressed in unfamiliar terms. Their vocabulary was forged long ago and may have lost some of its meaning and its dignity. Words like creation, sin, fall, incarnation, judgment, and faith are all pregnant with meaning but may need to be recast in terms that are more effective for reaching a broader, pluralistic world. Springing the traditional terms on one's audience will not be effective.

I think a more promising approach would be to argue *to religion* rather than *from religion*. That is, one could take up quite ordinary questions and show how soon they pushed on into issues of ultimacy, which is naturally the sphere of religion. This would reveal one's options, to see which seem more compelling. I gave some examples toward the end of my previous book. Such a method may seem more like ambush than like honest, frontal confrontation. But actually, it means that you and your conversation partner are more interested in discovery than in victory. Contests of worldviews point to victory, whereas probing assumptions seeks discovery. So this would embody a new academic etiquette.

I can't help thinking that a thorough discussion of naturalism, with its entirely nihilistic tendencies, would be a sobering exercise for the university. It stands behind so many of our crumbling ideologies that its chilling aspects would get the attention of the public in a way that few academic discussions have in recent years. For we probably can't live with the idea that "nature," as it is usually defined, finds no anchor for rights, dignity, human worth, fairness, commitment, service, or any of the values which we take entirely for granted. Naturalism once seemed to stand for liberation, but now it seems more like a loss of hope, an embrace of entropy.

*   *   *

16

But is there any reason to think that today's university will be receptive to talking about religion or entertaining religious perspectives? Paradigm changes are fiercely resisted, because they call one's training and previous career into question. Yet religion has forced itself into our consciousness in ways that would have surprised academics in the 1950s. It was impossible then to foresee that religion would reemerge in American politics in the 1970s. Much as some might regret the political forms it has taken, we can't ignore it. Second, it was impossible before the 1970s to foresee how world religions would upset our theories of modernization. The challenges to the existing world order require us to address religion.

Third, there has been a drastic change in our news product over the past fifty years ago. Back then journalists were too polite to mention religion. They would not have believed how much attention the news industry gives religion today. That industry has shifted more and more from the public to the private sphere, of course, but religion has moved from the private into the public sphere as well. This mingling of public and private spheres involves culture wars that always seem to have religious dimensions.

Fourth, within the university, postmodernism has meant a shaking of confidence in things like objective or rational proof. In the early twentieth century almost all disciplines looked to the sciences as their model. They declared their allegiance to the fact/value dichotomy, which supported secular approaches. Now that dichotomy is under philosophical scrutiny. Discovering that there are different "traditions of rationality," as Alasdair MacIntyre calls them, means that we must take responsibility for our judgments.[8]

The university's goal may no longer be proving people wrong so much as reaching understanding. There was a time when religious forces were the offenders in limiting debate. We are still stuck on that understanding of what religion *can* mean. Now it is secular forces that are in the censorship business, promoting a narrowing of debate.

*   *   *

8. Alasdair MacIntyre, *Whose Justice? Which Rationality?* (Notre Dame: University of Notre Dame Press, 1988).

The Western university has been through something like this collapse of confidence once before. It happened toward the end of the European Middle Ages. Scholars had tried to synthesize Christian and Greek philosophical traditions within a philosophical frame. They quarried scripture for propositions they could use in their theological edifice. It was a monumental effort but ended in failure, when the emerging nominalist philosophy convinced them that there were no self-validating rational principles at the basis of all thought. The resulting skepticism seemed inescapable and final. The academic logic they had done so much to develop let them down when they found that it could not spin truth out of itself. It raised doubts about the scholastic God of their own creating.

But the story doesn't end there. The exciting thing for Erasmus and other Christian humanists was the way religion came alive again when one abandoned the systematizing effort and allowed scripture its own narrative character. This was part of what fed into the reformations of religion and into an educational program that revived Western life. As you will see in these pages, we may be on the verge of something similar, with our emerging understanding of the role of discourse and of narrative as a method of investigation as well as description.

CHAPTER 2

Secularization Creates
the Corporate University

I F ONE can judge from media treatment, the American public is pretty well satisfied with its universities, except for sticker shock for attending the more prestigious ones. But satisfaction is definitely not the feeling of those who work in them. University professors are close to despair when they come up against the corporate methods that administrators now use to make things run more efficiently. According to Derek Bok, former president of Harvard, it was in the aftermath of the oil embargo crisis of the 1970s that the United States began to realize it would have to start economizing in many areas. And in the 1980s it became common to consult corporate managers and accountants to see what could be done to offer our universities' product at a cheaper rate. Bewildered educators are turning out numerous books lamenting this development.[1] We need to think about where this corporatizing came from, its essential meaning, its relation to secularization and to religion, and where we might place our hopes for a more humane future.

First, though, we should note what the public thinks of this situation. There have been two substantial opinion surveys taken to find the public's

---

1. Wesley Shumar, *College for Sale: A Critique of the Commodification of Higher Education* (Washington, D.C.: Falmer, 1997); Stanley Aronowitz, *The Knowledge Factory: Dismantling the Corporate University and Creating True Higher Education* (Boston: Beacon, 2000); David L. Kirp, *Shakespeare, Einstein, and the Bottom Line: The Marketing of Higher Education* (Cambridge, Mass.: Harvard University Press, 2003); Derek Bok, *Universities in the Marketplace: The Commercialization of Higher Education* (Princeton: Princeton University Press, 2003).

state of mind on our colleges. They show that we blame grades K-12 for any shortcomings in American education — even for college dropout rates. Higher education gets a free pass, apparently because it is associated with the business of America. Indeed, a president of the University of California recently proclaimed that "The business of the University of California is business."[2] In the ranking of its concerns, the public first wants university students to learn to be independent and mature, followed closely by the mastery of middle-class skills and credentials, and then to absorb some democratic virtues. "Exposure to great writers and thinkers" lagged considerably behind. Fourteen percent said it was "not too important," half (53 percent) thought it was "important, but not essential," leaving almost a third (32 percent) who thought it "essential." So the public is not disturbed by faculty attacks on the corporate model of education. After all, the university's new language of competition, marketing, profitability, development, publicity, investment, franchising, and management will make the "real world" familiar territory when students leave.

Thus the idea that universities are the priceless treasury of intellectual gold mined over several millennia is not a concern of the public. It trusts that somebody will stay behind to watch over that cultural treasury. Somebody we don't need to pay all that much.

The baby boomer generation is now aware that America will have to work to maintain any kind of economic leadership. And according to President Bok, the price of our new knowledge is going up steeply. In response to all this, federal and state governments have begun encouraging universities to become self-supporting, which means passing the costs along to "consumers." So we now see universities as primarily part of the economy.[3] Legislators may feel that it is only natural to shunt the burden of university support onto someone else. If they did not have any peak experiences in their humanities courses, they might not mind if professors squeal in protest.

I retired from a teaching career in a large state university that I truly enjoyed. I have not discouraged my son from preparing to do the same, and he is currently applying for a job as a professor. But he has a very

---

2. Quoted by David L. Kirp, in Richard H. Hersh and John Merrow, eds., *Declining by Degrees: Higher Education at Risk* (New York: Palgrave Macmillan, 2005), 114. Poll data is reported by Deborah Wadsworth, in *Declining by Degrees*, 23-38.

3. Bok, *Universities in the Marketplace*, 8-15.

good chance of getting no job at all, or of getting a part-time job without benefits that he will have to treat as an avocation. He is an Ivy League graduate who is much better prepared than I was when I broke into the profession so long ago.

What has happened in the last forty years to make things so bleak? At a recent session at an American Historical Association convention a thoughtful group of prominent speakers addressed the condition of the university in a panel on "Corporatizing Higher Education." Their general view was that if universities are modeled after business corporations, they will look very different from what we have been used to. Our culture may generally take the view that old is bad and new is good, but these prominent scholars thought that the new could be disastrous.

We used to think of universities as concerned with wisdom, which is seeing everything in its widest context. But when universities started, back in the Middle Ages, they were about vocational training. The church needed administrators and theologians; the emerging political states needed lawyers and judges and administrators; scholars knew about Greek and Roman medicine and wanted to pass that on; and there was a huge deficit of schoolteachers that could be filled by the products of these universities. But when the universities came into being, many of the students came to feel that they were intellectually exciting environments. Students were enjoying their teachers' debates over all sorts of philosophical questions. And they enjoyed the life of leisure, if you don't count schoolwork as real work. The medieval universities became quite popular, becoming a drag on the primitive economies of that day.

So as time went on, universities came to be thought of as bastions of intellectual life, about wisdom as much as vocation. Universities began to adopt the "humanistic" interests of the Renaissance. This meant trying to emulate the curiosity of the Greek and Roman aristocracies, who had ranked a study of wisdom with other upper-class pursuits like war and politics. The European aristocracy, which had previously left education to the church while they were fighting for control of a lawless situation, now decided that they wanted to pursue education, which meant that it acquired an aristocratic tone. In fact, after the Renaissance, the upper classes began to crowd out the lower ranks, who had been the main body of students before.

And so liberal education was re-started. The "liberal" in the title meant "free" — as in free men, those who would never have to work for a living, whose wealth and position and power were assured by birth. It seemed to these lucky ones that the proper use of their time was to study the wisdom of the past, the science and philosophy and theology that had been fostered by generations of medieval and ancient scholars. Education began to lose its professional character. We still recognize this appreciation for the liberal arts and sciences, although of course they have been transformed since then. To be liberally educated meant making sense of the life we humans have inherited and the world we find ourselves in.

But now we don't know how to fit such a program into our busy lives. The children of the boomer generation realize that nothing will be handed to them, and that they will have to work to maintain the same standard of living they were raised in. Women and men alike are now faced with this — everyone feels the need for job preparation.

For some time now, and without much debate on the subject, colleges and universities have allowed students more and more power to dictate what those institutions teach. We have emphasized freedom of choice to the point that students can put academic departments out of business by avoiding their offerings. Administrators may react by instituting requirements, but they seem almost apologetic about this. They are strongly averse to declaring that they can tell students what is good for them. Rather, they try to make their elective offerings more attractive in some way, especially by relating them to the "real world." We all understand this to mean the world of work, as if all worlds were not equally real.

Traditionally, it was assumed that universities need brilliant teachers to be teaching all these subjects, and that students need spare time to absorb and reflect on what they're getting. They are being dragged out of childhood into adulthood, and universities are our rite of passage. As part of this package, we needed to offer professors a decent salary so that they wouldn't be rejected by bourgeois society or distracted by necessity. In return, we expected them to give their whole lives to study, teaching, and writing.

For a long time, legislators tried to maintain this system in state schools. But universities have burgeoned, and there are many demands on public funds. In free countries, voters will have to be convinced of a need before they will support the raising of taxes. Unfortunately, the conviction that universities deserve what they are requesting has been eroding for a while now.

The story of the decline in monetary support for universities is a complicated one. It has to do with the relative position of this country as against the other economies in the world. It has to do with the feeling that professors and students might become lazy if we are too generous. That, in turn, comes from our society's elevation of hard work — obviously hard work — to such a high position among its values. It also has to do with the realization that the whole academic enterprise never had to pass a strict accounting of the resources they received, and it has to do with the increasing costs of scientific research that goes on within universities. Politicians want to see whether the public has supported their "start-up" for long enough that these institutions have become self-sufficient. Corporate organization seems the natural way to make them submit to standards of efficiency, the same way other professions do.

*　　*　　*

Everything I have just said has to do with money. It seems that the overriding reason for the trouble that universities are having is that money has risen to the top of our scale of values. We need to see how that relates to a secular culture and a decline in attention to "humanistic" values that were initially, and are still essentially, connected to religion.

First, what do I mean by a *scale* of values? Pretty much all societies have all the same values. But they don't arrange them, or rank them, in the same order. So societies end up looking and being very different, not because of different values but because of a different *ranking* of those values. Which values can trump other values when we need to choose? In some societies, honor would be the highest value; in some it would be religion; in others it might be leisure, or wealth, or family. All societies *have* all of these values, but they differ about which values should override the others. The scaling of values — arranging them in a scale — may change over time, but it changes very slowly, probably taking generations.

I'm counting on you to agree that the scale of values that we find in our media, our entertainment, our public discourse, has money at or close to the top. Money doesn't seem to have to justify itself (that is, in terms of some other even higher value). Of course, all through history there have been persons who were dominated by greed. But sometimes greed has seemed shameful compared to other values. What if greed became something to boast about? What if we found another word for it,

23

one that didn't make it sound so bad? People might argue that you weren't smart if you didn't do the "sensible" thing, making the decision that would bring you the most money. Or that you weren't smart if you didn't vote for those policies that promised the most monetary gain. But isn't this what has happened, with little or no notice being paid?

When we hear about the enormous salaries that some people get in our society, we might wonder whether this pursuit of money has become absurd. In the financial stratosphere, people apparently haggle over extra tens of millions of dollars. But if someone had a "salary" of 40 million dollars, what *meaning* would the 27th million have? The person would never see that 27th million, never spend it, never think about it, never enjoy it. It would do him or her absolutely no good, except to help in bragging. That 27th million *could* be vitally important if it went to someone who really needed it and could use it for something genuinely good.

The fact is that money is not a value at all. We hold money in reserve for when we discover something that really is of value — something money will make possible. But we have been misled into thinking that money itself is the value, is the good. Our other mistake is to think it is even a *measure* of all value, since so many real values cannot be purchased by money. We remind ourselves of this now and then, but are usually surprised when we think of it.

So I'm claiming that we *absolutize* money. It becomes an end in itself, and not a means to real ends. It's no longer related to needs, so we never feel we have enough of it. If one strategy promises more money than another, the argument is over. This keeps things simple, by giving us a universal measuring unit to measure jobs, companies, churches, policies, wines. Even universities are judged in monetary terms. What is their annual budget, or their endowment, or the average salary their graduates can earn, or the income from the patents they have produced, or the total of grants they have won this year?

Some have said that we "idolize" money, and this choice of words suggests that a theological analysis might be relevant. Professor Harvey Cox of Harvard Divinity School actually provided such a theological view of the subject in an article called "The Market as God."[4] When we discuss

---

4. Harvey Cox, "The Market as God," *Atlantic Monthly,* March 1999, 18-23. Cox credits Karl Polanyi's *The Great Transformation: The Political and Economic Origins of Our Time* (Boston: Beacon, 1957, orig. 1944) with the classic analysis of this situation.

our *ultimate* concerns, we're getting into the area in which theology operates well, so this may be the best way to think about it.

First, we need to acknowledge that markets have been a blessing for humanity when furthering humane values. But when they are allowed to become absolute rulers, markets can be monstrous. Market freedom is one value among many; market absolutism wipes out other values. Cox was interested in seeing the ways in which "the market" has become absolute — God, in his words.

Whether "God" is thought of as omnipresent, omnipotent, or omniscient, we find that in the purest capitalism, all of these adjectives remind us of the market, the place where money rules. *Omnipresence* means that nothing is outside the market's reach in commodification. There is now even a market in living cells. *Omnipotence,* in Cox's view, means the capacity to define what is real. And the market has that power, to translate "creation" into commodities, transubstantiating natural elements into saleable goods, to insure someone a profit. Finding a mate, mending a marriage, restorative leisure, certain natural views and sunsets — all these and more can be turned to someone's profit. Capitalism does this by sponsoring legal arrangements that fence potential customers off from nature's bounty. Unless this system were somehow limited by values coming from elsewhere, capitalism would have no problem with selling us into slavery. *Omniscience* is the comprehensive wisdom that transcends all human attempts to set such limits. The market's own mysterious processes set the exchanges between human labor, management, natural resources, and investment capital. To discern its wishes we watch the daily auguries from the stock markets. Trying to manipulate these matters for "human" ends would be something like a sin. And if sometimes bad things happen to good countries, we are assured that market discipline will bring a greater good. Not to any particular person, mind you, but to the market itself, which will forever transcend us. Interference with market mechanisms is treated like a kind of heresy. In all this, a certain reverence would not be out of place.

The point of theologizing this topic is to dramatize a fact that we may not have recognized: even our secular society is not without its absolute. But are we happy leaving money unchallenged in this way? Can this be squared with our other commitments? Shouldn't we reserve our ultimate reverence for something that takes the personal dimension into account?

As we mentioned in the first chapter, any absolute should be something that *personalizes* our ultimate values, as the doctrine of creation seems to do. Indeed, the so-called Anthropic Coincidences of cosmology seem to make this possible, which point to the contingency of "creation" — that is, the possibility that it might have happened differently.[5] The religions we are familiar with do enshrine personal values at the heart of their understanding of Being. The whole point of a Christian trinitarian theology, especially, is to show personality at the heart of reality.

*   *   *

There have been times in the past when human beings really did become commodities. We are proud of having put that time behind us. But the market is creeping back there, as body parts become commodities, like blood, kidneys, bone marrow, skin, sperm, eggs. We now hear of the harvesting of embryos for brain transplant tissue.[6] Apparently it requires fourteen living fetal brains for optimal results, though the amount of tissue required is small. They must be kept alive until they can be sacrificed. It is no surprise that newspapers avoid the subject for fear of inflaming public opinion.

When we had a more complex civilization there was a greater variety of values and we had to negotiate among them. Money and leisure and beauty and knowledge and health and responsibility and spirituality needed to be balanced against each other. Market dynamics have changed this over the past several centuries. When the level of market return is absolutized, we begin to feel we are its servants rather than its masters. At one time, the rights of capital had to justify themselves as against the other values we've just mentioned. But over the centuries business has brought us so many blessings that it has worn down our resistance.

It has become difficult to *argue* that natural beauty, or sustaining our environment, should trump a profitable enterprise, or that a broader and longer education might trump a quicker return to the world of jobs.

---

5. See the discussion of this subject in C. John Sommerville, *The Decline of the Secular University* (New York: Oxford University Press, 2006), 79-83.

6. Robert J. White, "Fetal Brain Transplantation: Questionable Human Experiment," *America* 167 (28 November 1992): 421.

Now our only way of slowing the pursuit of profit is through politics. We can *vote* against "development," but we no longer know how to argue against it successfully. We are hard pressed for arguments that trump profit or the freedom of capital. We can only defeat it with the force of blundering majorities, while the market can object that we didn't have a "reason" for our opposition.

This is where secularization comes into the picture. Religion anchored a lot of values besides money, like wisdom, responsibility, justice, love. It was generally suspicious of money, and now we see why. Almost all of our humane values are ultimately related to religion. Our very definitions of the human or humane were born in a religious discourse. Those definitions are in terms of our differences from our neighbors in nature, unlike definitions of *Homo sapiens,* which are in terms of our similarities. Thus, when religion began to be marginalized, money began its independent career. If we were to give up religion altogether, markets would reign supreme.

*　　　*　　　*

The secular research university has gotten caught up in the values of a secularized economy. As it declared its independence from religion in the twentieth century, it emphasized other ostensibly humane values like freedom, individualism, or science. But now money has become the measure of them all. Students all too often want the majors that promise the highest starting salaries. Faculty are eager to leave one college if they hear of a "better" job elsewhere. Administrators make their decisions with an eye to the financial advantage or security of their institutions. Taxpayers want the cheapest faculty available. Parents want the cheapest education on offer — unless they think a higher investment will guarantee an even higher return — and then too often wring their hands when they find out their children have chosen "impractical" majors.

The corporate model is essentially the view that the university has a product. The product is a degree, or more properly, the "human capital" holding that degree. Already in 1963 Clark Kerr, the chancellor of California's university system, was saying that the modern university's "product" was new knowledge.[7] Since then, there has been a general shift from

7. Aronowitz, *The Knowledge Factory,* 30.

discovery to application of knowledge. This ought to mean that the university should be attending to all the other values that our knowledge can serve, the human values we've been speaking of. Instead, its corporate character draws our attention to the one pseudo-value of money. For instance, the new knowledge still being gained by university research is now patented, with universities negotiating their cut of the royalties. Recently, before an important bowl game, I heard our football coach announce his confidence that the team would "put a good product on the field." We are losing the knack of talking about "education," which is a *process,* not a product.

Doubtless there are things that universities can learn from corporate practice. But this may not honor the essence of education. University presidents are now usually compared to corporate CEOs in their duties, and they are often brought in not from faculties, but from government or business. They don't necessarily come into their jobs with a clear vision of an educational ideal.

It is easily assumed that corporate-style leadership is needed to insure objective judgment. How do we know it is objective? Because it uses numbers. There are many things around a university that can be quantified: the number of applicants rejected, the number of student "consumers" a faculty "content provider" can process, the number of course hours needed to turn a freshman into a brain surgeon, the number of correct test answers that qualify students to skip whole years of an education, the retention rate, the graduation rate, the alumni giving rate. Putting all these numbers into a computer ostensibly produces the "rank" of your school.

When it is over, you don't brag about your education — you brag about your *degree,* and its market value in the real world. Years afterward, when the joy of making money begins to wane, you realize that graduation was *leaving* the real world. For college was the last chance you had to consider all of life.

*   *   *

These complaints would be echoed by many faculty. But what arguments can they offer that would get the *public's* attention? We do sometimes limit market dynamics to something that we can live with. But how do we argue for tempering them? First we may find someone to blame. Professors may blame politicians, forgetting that they had those politicians in class and failed to make them wise. Or they may blame students, who are too young to appreciate a rounded education and are eager to find that first serious job. Faculties may lament the passing of old-style social- or welfare-capitalism, which argued from ideas of social responsibility and justice. But have they been explaining these values in their own teaching or writing? Have they been maintaining the moral and even religious bases of those values?

The very idea of the university doesn't make sense outside of a social, cultural, and ethical structure — what we used to call a civilization. Universities have always implied the right of society to participate in knowledge and share in the power that it offers. So they have always been motivated by humane values. But we have been testing the bottom for a long time now, seeing how far we can allow freedom, irresponsibility, individualism, and acquisitiveness to proceed before reining them in. When we have had enough, we may find that we have forgotten the arguments that could be used against them.

From time to time, we *vote* to curb corporate excesses. But if there is little argument involved, our votes will not carry the needed conviction. Reasons will be chosen haphazardly. In a proudly secular culture we are awkward about arguing the human good. We may never have learned how arguments about "justice" go. We're afraid not everyone will agree, because we now assume that value terms just refer to people's *feelings.* So we simply count heads instead of looking for what is *in* them.

Could we find arguments that would bring agreement? Would we find them in the university — in the philosophy department, perhaps? Or religious studies, or the business school, or the law school? Or are these departments part of the problem? Even humanities departments, which were once charged with keeping alive a sense of the "best" that had been thought, said, and done, are becoming departments of cultural studies, whose job is to uncover the *pretensions* of past cultures.

The one area we will not consult is religion. It seems to have too much baggage from the past. It dredges up profound disagreements and, if not handled properly, offers few ways to resolve them. Yet religions are, more or less by definition, one's ultimate terms of reference. All arguments must end somewhere, and the non-negotiable ground of your assumptions and arguments will constitute your religious commitments, whether you thought you had a religion or not. The alternative is to have no convictions and no personal core. Arguing from a recognized religious basis doesn't mean that you are forcing others to accept your religion. It means you are asking them to see if they can counter it in a substantive way. The secular university began by assuming that rationalism provided the universal language which could resolve such basic questions. When that proved not to be true, it decided to ignore the questions.

If universities were serious about countering some of the economic and corporate pressures on them, they might have to learn how to argue with conviction from alternative values. They might build some measure of agreement on the basis of what philosopher John Rawls called an overlapping consensus. Given the various "traditions of rationality" that Alasdair MacIntyre describes, this will involve religious voices. Philosophers are no longer pressing the dichotomy of facts and values, and that might open the way for serious debates.[8]

*   *   *

Ideologies like "market society" can seldom be identified as ideologies by those inside them. They are more likely to be recognized by outsiders. Religion these days is obviously in the position of an outsider to the secular university, which may help it to make a contribution of this sort. Indeed, at basis, religions witness to something outside all cultural forms, which is defined as "transcendent." There have been times when religious institutions became socially and culturally dominant, and thoroughly institutionalized. Most would agree that those were not its best days. Religion seems to be better in the role of cultural critic and might be of great value in the debate needed in the university today.

It may be, as I mentioned earlier, that the traditional opposition between religion and "humanism" is a thing of the past. They are natural allies in adopting a personalist stance. "Secular humanism" flirted with philosophical naturalism in trying to win its independence from religion. But they are strange bedfellows. If the recovery of essential educational practices means a recovery of some kind of humanism, we can remind ourselves that the Renaissance began in a Christian humanism. Most of the public, including the government, might begin to under-

8. See the critique in Sommerville, *Decline of the Secular University,* chapter 3.

stand the criticisms of market hegemony if they were put in the religious and human terms they are familiar with.

We need to recognize, however, that religion needs the university's intellectual forum as much as the university needs religion's seriousness about values. Having access to university debates should encourage religion's better self. It could be an important source of the kind of self-criticism that would be beneficial to all of society and culture.

Secular academics have attempted other forms of critique of our corporatization, but without much success. That convention panel I mentioned put its hopes in unionization. That is, they thought the economic interests of downtrodden academics was the likeliest answer to an opposite set of economic imperatives. Obviously they were having a hard time finding traction for arguments within a secular framework. Perhaps that is because the secular culture is more the problem than the solution.

Harvard professor Howard Gardiner has recently observed that educational success might be best measured by how well students can analyze and critique the corporate model of education.[9] That is, true intellectual sophistication would require the market model to justify itself. But where would students, or their professors, find the values to anchor their critique? If students achieved some such perspective, they would also have learned something of their own faith — that is, their personal and intellectual orientation, the source of their values and hopes.

9. In Hersh and Merrow, *Declining by Degrees,* 109.

31

CHAPTER 3

Defining Religious and
Secular Arguments

T HE NOTION of introducing religious arguments in secular universities will probably cause one of two reactions: one is to view it as preposterous; the other is to see it as frightening. It has been so long since
religion has engaged our academic attention that we may not be able to
imagine the scenario. Yet I will argue that quasi-religious arguments are
very prevalent in our so-called secular institutions. To recognize them,
and to see how unavoidable they are, we need to begin with some definitions — of "religious" and "secular," of course, but also of the concepts of
"science," "spirituality," and "human."

What all of these terms have in common is that they can only be defined nominally rather than referentially. They are not words that refer to
"things"; they are concepts that must be defined before we can identify
the "things" intended. This points to the two main kinds of definition:
nominal, and "real" or referential. Referential definitions are suitable
when everyone would agree on the things the term was *referring* to.
Nominal or semantic definitions, by contrast, are the definitions of
words. In all of the cases mentioned above, there is some doubt as to
what all actually fits the definition. They don't denote things that can be
grasped, but are concepts that guide our thinking.

In the case of religion, we don't know whether a particular institution or activity or belief merits the description as religious unless we
know what "religious" *means*. We don't know what a humane value is until we know what "human" means. We don't know whether some old and
doubtful fact is scientific until we've decided how the term "science" is

32

properly used. Likewise with the definitions of "secular" and "spiritual." In English, they are both currently defined in opposition to "religious," so we will need to define "religious" before we can distinguish them.[1]

If we are to argue that even the secular university cannot do without religious arguments, we will need to show what religious arguments look like, and how such arguments improve the university's ability to address our problems.

*   *   *

There is good reason for our contemporary confusion over the terms "religion" and "religious." Since the late eighteenth century, the West has become aware of some of the world's other faiths or worldviews, and has tended to extend its term "religion" to many of them. Scholars in the field of religious studies caution us that we can't assume that our English word "religion" really fits them all. They go ahead and use the term, even in their department title, but they may complain that even football gets tagged as a religion. Even scholars of religion run into trouble when they insist on giving the word a real or referential definition. Comparative religion may aspire to be something like a science, and it is a requirement of a science that it give referential definitions to its subjects, so that everyone is agreed on what exactly they are studying. If religious studies settled for defining the *word* instead, they would be admitting that they are only defining an English word. They would be admitting that their definition was culture-specific, and Western. It would imply that other cultures might have different words or a different shading to a similar concept. But what's wrong with that? We talk a lot about respecting diversity, and that means acknowledging the differences in our languages, concepts, and mentalities. It is better to acknowledge that some cultures didn't have anything that exactly corresponded to what English-speakers call religion than to extend our empire by colonizing their experience under our particular terms.

Sciences aspire to universal languages, like mathematics, which all cultures can understand in the same way. So each science is a language. But in the wider culture, no one just speaks Language without speaking any particular language. And it is well known that our English word "reli-

---

1. On all these points, see C. John Sommerville, *Religion in the National Agenda: What We Mean by Religious, Spiritual, Secular* (Waco: Baylor University Press, 2009).

gious" is sometimes of doubtful meaning. For example, we sometimes speak loosely of rituals, cults, beliefs, liturgies, commandments, and so forth, that are *not* religious, though we normally think of such things as religious. How do we know which are and which aren't? How do English speakers make that distinction?

Apparently, the way we do it — the way we define these terms — is to compare them with other terms that are close in meaning. With reference to "religious," we would contrast it to a wide range of terms, from "spiritual" or "mystical" to "creed" or "sect," to "worship" or even "idolize," to show the slight differences that justify those other terms. This is all we can do. We can't identify all the actual examples of religion for a referential definition *before* we've determined what "religion" means. This is behind the problem of whether certain kinds of Buddhism or Confucianism, say, are religions, philosophies, worldviews, spiritualities, or something else.

All this has nothing to do with whether religion is real or not. It is at least as real as science is real. Science is a concept, used for those assumptions, beliefs, theories, and practices that guide a certain kind of thought and activity. Science does not reside in the physical things it describes, but in the descriptions of their relations. It is the same with religion.

Those who study religion are aware that the various things they describe as religions may have very little in common. Some may not have gods, or afterlives, or cosmologies, or even what would look like ethical systems to us. One response to this fact is to insist that while all these various "religions" do not have common *elements*, they do have common *functions*. Usually this is put in terms of the social cohesion that religions offer, or in their overarching explanations or symbolization of life.

There is no doubt that religions do have functions, or they would not be as widespread or persistent as they are. Scholars have often hoped that finding common functions would help provide a sense of the essence of religion while avoiding the necessity of approving or disapproving judgments, which is congenial to the scientific approach. But one cannot, in fact, define religion functionally, for several reasons.

For example, the clearest examples of what we call religions have sometimes been not sources of social cohesion but rather dysfunctional, disruptive forces, splitting societies between rival faiths.[2] Beyond that,

2. For example, Victor W. Turner, *The Ritual Process: Structure and Anti-Structure*

students of religious ritual have sometimes concluded that these have no ulterior function, no end beyond themselves — like play, except that one cannot lose.[3] In any event, it is not clear that religions serve the same functions in every society, or that functions remain the same through time. Any of these objections mean that while functions may characterize some religions some of the time, they are not essential or defining.

But the biggest problem with functional definitions is that they are not specific. That is, they are apt to place religion into larger categories along with the other things that serve the same function. If the essential purpose of religion were social bonding, for example, it might be included along with other things that helped toward that end. This confuses the issue; should one extend the term "religion" loosely to everything in that category, or are we differentiating the religious element from its functional equivalents by some implicit definition of the religious? Such an implicit definition would need to be examined, and it would turn out to be substantive rather than functional.

The point is that a definition should, if possible, identify unique aspects of a word, and functional definitions do not. Of course, religion can *have* many functions — explanatory, expressive, ethical, existential. We are only saying that these functions are not its *defining* characteristic.

Elsewhere, I traced a path of discovery to the definition of "religion" or "religious," which is too long for the space available here.[4] In brief, I found "religious" to be *the word we use for a certain kind of response to a certain kind of power, the kind of response and the kind of power both understood to be beyond anything else in our experience.* The noun form, "religion," would therefore be a particular formulation of the response and the power being considered. The adverb, "religiously," would qualify the manner in which those activities were undertaken.

You may think that this can't be right, because you know of some religions that don't fit that scheme. They simply are not religions in the English sense of the term. The practice of missionaries and anthropologists

---

(Chicago: Aldine, 1969), 4, where Turner alludes to "the extreme importance of religious beliefs and practices, for both the maintenance and radical transformation of human social and psychical structures."

3. Frits Staal, "The Meaninglessness of Ritual," *Numen* 26 (1979): 2-22.

4. C. John Sommerville, "Resurrecting Religion in a New (Hermeneutical) Dimension," *Fides et Historia* 30 (1998): 21-30, and rejoinder to critics in 31 (1999): 167f. This is expanded in the work cited in note 1 of this chapter.

in calling them religions is recent, and has not actually changed English usage. Granted, even the most scholarly treatments of Asian "religions" always have to mention that there are problems involved in using our common understanding of religion for them, but that often becomes a way of simply waving the problem away. One must go by the particular rules of the language one is speaking — and few of us speak Comparative Religion. So while other practices may be close to our meaning of religion, we should be able to note their differences without fear of seeming disrespectful or provincial.

*   *   *

Before going on to our other terms, we need to ask how this definition of religion is likely to affect the intellectual arguments that might engage the university. After all, the definition seems so abstract that it doesn't suggest any particular doctrines. The bare definition does not specifically mention God or any duties or understandings that we associate with our familiar religions.

But that is precisely the point. The university can recognize something as a religious argument even though it does not get into any of the most characteristic doctrines of a particular religion. For religion goes deeper than particular doctrines. Major religious traditions show how particular understandings of ultimate reality (or power) permeate the whole of a culture. But they begin at a level so basic that we may not associate them with something like, say, salvation. I've been saying that "creation," "human," and a range of humane values are anchored in religions as we have defined the term. It is unfortunate that too many academics' last brush with religion was in childhood, when they had only a rudimentary understanding of the matter. They may never have learned the mental structure that their own birthright religion depends upon, or be able to see how their present assumptions relate to it. I hope to give examples in the chapters to follow.

*   *   *

The first contrast we can consider is in reference to the term "spiritual." The current popularity of the word is evidence that the word "religion" is not as elastic as some people would argue, and that the public has realized the need to bring another word into the discussion. As we experience problems defining "religion," people would rather use a different term than to stretch this one entirely out of shape.

Wade Clark Roof interviewed California baby boomers on their religious or spiritual quests, and noted their preference for the term "spirituality." Though they were hazy on the term, he gathered that they meant a rejection not so much of religion as of organized or institutional religion, which seemed lifeless and external. Having been disappointed with churches, it excited them to think that spirituality could indicate something more personal. They embraced spirituality as part of their identity "against a background of fragmentation and commodification of the self in modern society."[5]

Roof noticed that those who use this term don't like defining it, since a central feature of the experience is a questing mentality: "The spiritual comprehends but cannot be contained by intellect, cognition, or institutional structure; it reaches out for unity and the ordering of experience; it abhors fixity in the interest of transformation."[6] Robert Wuthnow found much the same in a study of artists who were identified as expressing "spiritual" interests in their work. He noted that they were drawn to the term in reaction against the technical, rational, and commercial character of modern society. But they also reported being in reaction against organized religion. Spirituality connoted something more intrinsic or personally authentic. It also helped that spirituality was not subject to the philosophical or moral criticisms directed at historical religions. Other scholars report similar findings.[7]

Note that spirituality does not seem to require the same kind of ethical or existential "response" as religion does. We may conclude that, in current usage, spirituality is more like an aesthetic category. Without an ethical dimension, it appears to be an apprehension, like our feeling for beauty. There may be no commitment involved.

---

5. Wade Clark Roof, *Spiritual Marketplace: Baby Boomers and the Remaking of American Religion* (Princeton: Princeton University Press, 1999), 35, 44, 81. See also Robert C. Fuller, *Spiritual, But Not Religious* (New York: Oxford University Press, 2001), 5.

6. Roof, *Spiritual Marketplace*, 34.

7. Robert Wuthnow, *Creative Spirituality* (Berkeley: University of California Press, 2001), 7. See also Brian J. Zinnbauer, Kenneth I. Pargament, et al., "Religion and Spirituality: Unfuzzying the Fuzzy," *Journal for the Scientific Study of Religion* 36 (1997): 549-64; Wade Clark Roof, *A Generation of Seekers* (San Francisco: Harper, 1993), 76f.

The fact that neuroscientists are eager to study the mental states of spirituality is an unconscious recognition of its aesthetic and psychological character. Like the rest of us, neuroscientists must identify the subjects of their study linguistically. Nerve impulses don't come labeled "religious," "spiritual," "secular," or "scientific." The scientists must go by our common language use in setting up their studies. The impulses they study as instances of spirituality must be identified as such before they can argue that they are studying spirituality rather than something else.

If we define spirituality as an aesthetic category, then it could obviously be subject to neurological study. Impulses or feelings are just the sort of thing that might register physically. So spirituality is precisely the part of our subject that could, in principle, be reduced to physicalist concepts.

Religion, on the other hand, involves more than that spiritual impulse. The ethical or existential judgment or response involved creates greater difficulties for scientific naturalism. Just as neuroscience will never explain *itself,* never explain the intentions of scientists or the truth value of their statements in terms of neural impulses, it cannot encompass religion itself, as we have defined it. For religion has that area of *response* to consider in addition to the *awareness* that it shares with spirituality.

Spirituality need not detain us in our discussions. It makes no intellectual claims, just as mysticism has built no intellectual structures for purposes of argument. This may be a relief to those who do not want to have to justify their spiritual awareness in intellectual terms.

*   *   *

Secular ideas are defined negatively, as the absence of religious concerns. This derives from "secular's" core meaning of a separation of ideas or activities from religious associations or direction. In ordinary English, such separation can take any of five forms. In reviewing these different meanings, we can show that they correspond to common usage of very long standing, as evidenced in the *Oxford English Dictionary* (OED).

1. When discussing social structures — or "societies" with regard to their structures or symbol systems — secularization is used to mean *differentiation.* In this case, secularization means the separation of religious activities, groups, or ideas from others present in the society. According to the OED, since the thirteenth century English usage has included such

phrases as "secular rulers," "secular judges," "secular lords," or "secular historians" to mean those who have no connection with the "church." It does not mean that these rulers, judges, etc., were personally non-religious. It only means they lack an official connection to religious institutions due to such differentiation.

When the general public uses the term "society," it usually does not mean the social structure, but rather the *population* contained within that structure. That creates an ambiguity that we will discuss below. Nevertheless, the public understands that there are autonomous activities and institutions, differentiated from religion in the sense of being free from religious direction or association, and in that sense "secular." Many of these activities once did have a connection to religious organizations in the West, but there were processes of differentiation that cut them loose, as when some university scholars lost all connection with the churches that had once fostered all universities.

2. When discussing *institutions,* we use "secularization" to mean the *transformation* of an institution that had once been considered religious in character into something not thought of as religious. This is also the sense in which we speak of the secularization of objects that were once associated with religion but which lost that connection. It is easy to think of examples of such things, like the European university or church property. The OED lists an English example from 1570 to refer to Henry VIII's secularization of the monastic lands. The clergy and monks that lost their jobs in the church at that time were also said to have been "secularized" — which, again, did not mean that they lost their religious faith.

3. When discussing *activities,* "secularization" is taken to mean the *transfer* of activities from institutions of a religious nature to others without that character. The list of such activities is longer than one may think. For nothing is intrinsically secular; anything whatever can be considered as part of one's religion, including cooking, dancing, agriculture, military technology, or even keeping time.[8] One would refer to the early modern transfer of welfare services from the church to the state as the secularization of that function. So we can now speak of secular literature, for example, without intending any challenge to religion.

4. When discussing *mentalities,* we take "secularization" to mean a

---

8. C. John Sommerville, *The Secularization of Early Modern England: From Religious Culture to Religious Faith* (New York: Oxford University Press, 1992).

significant shift of attention from the ultimate concerns of religion to more proximate ones. The secularization of mentality can, of course, take a more decided turn against religion, in active doubt or open disbelief. As early as 1395 the OED records a mention of the clergy's "secular affections," to indicate wayward or worldly beliefs.

5. As mentioned above, the secularization of a society is not the same thing as the secularization of a population. For social scientists, "society" means a structure (or even a process) rather than the persons contained within that structure. So we can quite properly speak of a secular society which contains a largely religious population. That would mean that the rules under which such a society operates are recognized as having a different character from the religious beliefs held by the population. On the other hand, where a whole population is characterized by a neglect of religious habits or convictions, one might speak of the secularization of that population, which would be a generalization of the fourth usage above. Most of our present confusion on the subject of secularization is due to this ambiguity in the term "society" — whether we mean the role-structure or those filling the roles.

The term "secularism" can be differentiated from these processes of secularization. It dates from around 1852 and describes an ideology organized to complete and enforce secularization.

*   *   *

Since "secular" is only defined negatively, as the absence of religion, there can be several different secular mentalities. To be specific, we would have to identify which positive viewpoints we have in mind: naturalistic, rationalistic, pragmatic, historicist, utilitarian, materialistic, romanticist, existentialist, and many other perspectives, supporting a range of theories and arguments. At about the time of the French Revolution, when the intellectual and social position of Christian religion was first challenged in a major way, ideologies were formulated on the basis of such worldviews. Ideologies such as Liberalism, Conservatism, Socialism, Utilitarianism, Racism, Nationalism, Social Darwinism, Fascism, and Communism have followed each other. Their job was to replace religions, which were thought to be failing. Like religions, they offered comprehensive intellectual perspectives as well as the emotional and ethical resources which could form the basis for social and individual life.

Ideologies, in this sense, were the convincing assumptions that might bind society's ideas, explanations, goals and hopes together. They were what we might call faiths. If we define "faith" as one's basic intellectual and personal orientation, the source of one's values and hopes, then it is obvious that people cannot live without some such thing. Many looked to these quasi-religious cultures to provide the assurance and the motivation to keep society moving ahead. Some of these ideologies even found room for traditional religions in a supporting role.

The twentieth century was hard on all these substitute faiths, as they disappointed their followers in one way or another. Of these various approaches, the strongest remaining are naturalism, the faith as well as the method of many scientists, and liberal capitalism, which tries to tame the market ideology we discussed in the last chapter. We also notice that religion has survived even in the West, though more as a personal stance than as a social ideology. Given the incoherence of our intellectual culture, we may look to any of these for useful elements. The ideology of *secularism* is strongly associated with science. It strikes many as the antithesis of religion, or as its replacement — the stance of those who want to see the influence of religion reduced.

*   *   *

Science is another of those matters that must be defined nominally, rather than referentially. One might think that science amounts to the list of all those discoveries that scientists have announced in the past. If that were so, a referential definition would be possible, amounting to that list of true facts and theories. But as we know, science often has to revise its view of things, and the history of science embraces mistakes that scientists might now reject with scorn. So science is typically defined in terms of its methods rather than its results. The debate over just what that "method" amounts to has become quite complicated. There are as many particular methods as there are sciences, and some would say that each research question and experiment requires its own method, parts of which are only understood tacitly even by the researcher.[9] So defining "science" must now involve broad notions of principle.

9. See Michael Polanyi, *Personal Knowledge: Towards a Post-Critical Philosophy* (London: Routledge, 1958).

Obviously, "science" cannot simply mean "truth," since some of what counted as scientific truth in past centuries has been superseded or transformed by later claims. One could protest that those earlier attempts were not really science if they weren't true. But then we cannot be sure that what scientists are saying today will prove to be the last word. Since those previous propositions were arrived at by something we can recognize as a scientific program, we can honor them as scientific statements even though they may have been overturned.

Thus science is understood in opposition to other, less rigorous methods of inquiry. This is the way of nominal definition. And there is another sense in which it is understood nominally. Cultures differ in the subjects they consider to be sciences. Whether one includes sociology, psychoanalysis, or linguistics among the sciences is a matter of convention. Some cultures even include history or literary criticism, which would make the question of the relation of "science" and religion quite different. This is not to say that scientific knowledge is socially constructed, but that the *concept* of science is.

Science as systematic study will involve the fact that it is open to replication and verification — or falsification — by others who will take the trouble. The methods used must be explicit, and "scientific proof" amounts to getting the agreement of those who are acknowledged to be in a position to judge. Things are proved so long as those who are in a position to judge agree that they are proved.

Crucial to this replication is that the things being studied are "real" in the common-sense meaning of always being there when one wants to study them. This suggests a problem when science offers to study religion. Will the putative "object" of religion hold still long enough to be studied under controlled conditions? One might say that the reason science can't study religion is precisely because it is not real in this physical sense. But things can be real in other ways. Religious thinkers could appeal to the fact that philosophers do not think it meaningful to speak of what is *real in general.*[10] Concepts are real if they cannot be "reduced" to lower levels of analysis without remainder.

Scientific "reduction" (i.e. explanation) occurs when the realities of

10. Alfred Schutz, "On Multiple Realities," in *Collected Papers* (Hague: Nijhoff, 1962-66), 1:209-59, and Thomas Nagel, *Mortal Questions* (Cambridge: Cambridge University Press, 1979), 211.

one science, like economics, can be entirely accounted for at the level of social psychology, or when psychology is accounted for at the level of biochemistry. This is not as easy as it may seem. Each level of "reality" — each science, let's say — has elements that are entirely real to the other elements of that level but lose their meaning entirely when analyzed in the terms of a "more basic" one. Things can be "real to each other" that simply don't register at the sub-atomic level. So "reduction" is not of objects, but of theories and concepts. It is subsuming one explanatory theory within a more comprehensive one. A religion which claimed to be a science, expressing itself in theories, would place itself in danger of such treatment.[11] But in our nominal usage, religion is recognized as quite different from this.

Some sciences have made efforts to explain religion, or explain it away. They do not mean the *object* of religion — that transcendent power we have spoken of — but rather religious *behavior*. So it is religious *persons* who are being studied, and not the essence of the thing. The most obvious approaches are through sociology (which has seen religion as a society's representation and glorification of itself), psychology (which may see it as a residue of infantile fears), and more recently rational-choice economics (which applies cost/benefit analysis to the behavior). None of them touch the core of religion, but only religious behaviors, ideas, practices, or attitudes. They are often successful in this — without dissolving the reality of the concept.

On the other hand, religion can offer its own explanation of science. The fact that only humans cultivate science shows a characteristic human interest in understanding and truth, and in transcending the world we find ourselves in. It is one of those activities that prove the reality of purpose and personal categories within the universe. To explain scientific activity naturalistically would be absurd, like finding a sociobiological explanation of sociobiology itself. If we found one, it would therefore cease to be "true," because "true" would consequently have no meaning. Science would just be a product of evolution, like fingers. We don't speak of fingers as "true."

Religions have attempted to explain science as an effort to complete what theology has begun — a study of God's other reality. This was the

---

11. Hans H. Penner, *Impasse and Resolution: A Critique of the Study of Religion* (New York: Peter Lang, 1989), 23f.

case with some prominent scientists of the past, like Copernicus, Kepler, Boyle, and Newton. More recent scientists have often expressed the same sense of following a Creator whose cunning and even wit astonishes them. Einstein left many such references, and they are familiar among today's cosmologists.[12]

*   *   *

Finally, we come back to the subject of defining the human. This, of course, is where religious arguments will be most familiar, and most important within the university. They will also be unavoidable. It would be very awkward and self-conscious to argue over the human good without referring to the different bases of those arguments, the different assumptions and faiths that ground them. Naturalism, which has been such a fruitful methodological assumption in the sciences, has been drawn into this area, where it is inconclusive. Definitions of Homo Sapiens show where we fit within the range of biological species, but we know intuitively that this is not an exhaustive account.

Definitions should tell both how things resemble other things *and* how they differ. Oddly enough, declaring what we understand ourselves to be can be *more* definite than defining *Homo sapiens.* The science involved in studying *Homo sapiens* is always indefinite, since species may change over time or vary geographically or show individual variations. They seem like approximations.

It might be objected that different cultures also define the human differently. We may imagine that all adequate definitions must be universal. But even if some cultures did not notice a human difference from the rest of creation, surely they all assume personal concepts that are associated with humans, and only with humans. If there is any cultural complexity at all, they seek to understand values like justice, wealth, responsibility, and so on. Finding a culture that lacked such concepts would not call ours into question. If we met extra-terrestrials who had entertained no religious concepts, we could doubt that we had met with intelligent life.

What this means is that in defining the human or the humane, we are proceeding hermeneutically. That is, we are interrogating our own under-

12. See C. John Sommerville, *The Decline of the Secular University* (New York: Oxford University Press, 2006), chapter 6.

standings of the matter and the understandings of others. We might think that proceeding along the lines of anatomy would be more precise, less problematic. More than that, we fear that trying to understand humans, rather than merely describe them, will inevitably get us into normative judgments. We will begin talking of norms or values, and there will be disagreement. Indeed, our definition of the human will itself be a value, as in our term "humane," which holds up the human as something to aspire to. The problem is that we cannot avoid this. We can't help arguing over the truer meaning of the humane values, of the best sense of what is just, true, or loving. Ethics belongs in the university. We can't pretend to be satisfied with values clarification, let alone the dismissal of values in line with the entirely questionable fact/value dichotomy.

We fail in our duty to discuss the human in its ethical aspects when we medicalize the deviance of those who violate humane values. There is nothing wrong with giving what help we can to the violators, but that cannot be the whole of the story. So while it may sound like the empirical approach deals in biological reality while a hermeneutic approach deals only in ideas, we must realize that there is nothing unreal about ideas. Science itself is an idea. If evolutionary psychology had been successful in reducing *all* value terms to behaviorist ones, it would have destroyed the foundations of science itself as a search for a meaningful truth. Thus we are justified in using both of these approaches to defining ourselves, depending on the questions we want to answer.

Scholars may object that definitions of the human are "essentialist," robbing humans of the very existential freedom that they think *defines* us. Or that they think *should* define us, in their own ethical prescription. Any definition of the human useful to our professional programs will naturally speak to the optimal for humans. It will be normative, reminding us of our best nature. It will invite judgment on those who violate it, whether they be politicians or the more usual suspects. So long as universities exist to discuss the issues of human life, we will keep rediscovering ethics at the heart of university instruction and research.

The other temptation will be to think that "philosophy" can substitute for religion, as less controversial and less dated. Bringing up the Greeks and Romans does not get us away from religion, which was never far from their thoughts. Christian theology was able to use their insights for that reason, finding the ultimate reference that their thinking seemed to lack.

*   *   *

What does all of this suggest for the future of academic discussion? Mostly I have tried to show a greater complexity in this area than we may have assumed. Secularity does not come in only one flavor any more than religion does. Bits of many ideologies and of older religious views still circulate on our campuses. Outside of philosophy departments, the taxonomy of our arguments would not be readily apparent. And philosophy majors are an endangered species.

We have not offered obvious ways of categorizing religious as against secular arguments. It will not be easy to discriminate between them — an important point, by the way. Most generally, those which deal with ultimate resolutions or commitment thereby reveal a religious element. And the most rigorously nihilistic will be secular, and offer the greatest challenge to the religious. Those arguments that are somewhere in between can only be sorted out by courteous debate.

Censoring arguments once gave religious institutions a bad name. Defining religions as censors in order to justify censoring them, however, is just as bad. To appeal to "tolerance" in order to silence religious voices that not everyone shares is to fail to recognize that there is *nothing* that everyone shares.

What we need is a new sense of when ideas have won the right to be heard. The academic gatekeepers need new criteria, now that rationalism of the old sort has itself been problematized. But in our increasingly diverse world, the contributions of religious voices will need to take a new form. Those who have only a caricature of religion may suppose that religious people will start from unfamiliar religious metaphors or concepts, such as "redemption" or "incarnation" or "God" or "damnation," and pit them against more familiar secular concepts. But instead of arguing from some fully developed religious doctrines, new religious voices might be more successful by taking up some seemingly ordinary question or paradox that was giving us problems, to show how rapidly it raised ultimate questions. These are the questions that leave one at the point of decision, where one's faith is revealed. There is nothing to keep tax-supported universities from exploring the whole range of answers available, whatever their source. If religions offer the most intuitively convincing views, they would deserve to be explored rather than dismissed by some secular prohibition.

46

Universities are now about choices as much as they are about answers — how to apply our knowledge as much as how to increase it. Choices reveal our basic pre-theoretical orientation. Among at least some theologians and philosophers today, faith is taken to mean something like *our basic intellectual and personal orientation, the source of our values and hopes.* There are secular faiths, of course, in the absence of self-validating rational principles. We need to become more adept at speaking across the gaps, acknowledging each other's faiths.

We are led to believe, by Kurt Gödel's famous Incompleteness Theorem, that even mathematical systems must be completed by some principle outside that system. It reminds us that the medieval science of theology was "faith seeking understanding," which was only paraphrasing St. Augustine's "Unless you believe, you shall not understand."[13] They did not mean belief being satisfied with belief. Rather, they knew that we have to break into any rationality through something like a basement door.

For Augustine the goal was the understanding, not just the believing. Belief is not an end in itself, but gives us the patience to reach a greater understanding. And religious faith is something bigger than belief. Faith has to sustain not simply one's intellect or understanding, but also one's commitments and hopes. Given our different religious and secular faiths, no particular one will ever dominate the university. But they could be allowed to make their contribution to the practical questions of our academic as well as our political and social lives.

13. Polanyi, *Personal Knowledge,* 266.

CHAPTER 4

Why Christianity and Secularization Need Each Other

T HERE IS more to the issue of religion and secularity than the opposition implied in the definition of "secular." In fact, I'm going to argue something surprising: I believe secularization provides the scenario that makes sense of religion, or at least of Christianity. We have been insisting that American culture needs something more than the secular to thrive. But we need to see that religion needs to respect a sphere that is not religion as well.

If secularization is most generally the separation of things from religious associations or direction, Christianity, at least, can live with that. *Secularism,* of course, would be different, being the effort to complete secularization — and enforce it. As another of the nineteenth-century ideologies it has never been a dominant force, except in the erstwhile Soviet sphere. But we shall see that secularization is something that was acknowledged by the time of the writing of Deuteronomy, in the Jewish Torah, and that a measure of secularization provided the environment in which the Christian church was born and prospered. Christianity, perhaps uniquely among major religions, thrives within a secular world.

We naturally think of secularization as religion's enemy, and in a sense it is. It means limiting religion by removing areas of activity and thought from the sphere of religion's direction or influence. But we may also think of secularism as an enemy of the secular, in robbing society of the kind of inspiration and leadership that societies require. In the case of universities I have argued that relentless secularization reduces them to trade schools, even though we like to imagine them to be something more. When universities were transformed into secular institutions a little over a hundred years ago, they didn't realize they had cut their lifeline to ultimate sources of meaning, but now it is becoming more and more apparent.

Some religious critics of the secular university may take its secularity for granted and plead for a niche within the academy as it exists. Clearly a comprehensive academic culture would involve both religious and non-religious voices, and benefit from their interaction. Indeed, the modern university began with such debates, though the debates soon withered away. A regeneration of the university would not only help the university, but could mean an intellectual recovery for religion as well. Religion has been told for so long that it has no intellectual dimension that it has begun to believe it. But some religions, at least, do best in a secular environment. In fact, it's the only setting in which they thrive.

Christianity has been most true to itself when it can compare itself to the secular. It is most itself when seen against a backdrop of the meaningless or the hopeless. Ancient historian Robert A. Markus has explored the church's early acknowledgment of a secular realm, especially by St. Augustine. As Markus puts it, Christianity introduced the concept of the secular into a Roman world that knew only the very different dichotomy of sacred and profane. Profane meant contempt for the sacred, not the indifference that secular denotes. Augustine formulated and even defended a place for the secular realm in the divine plan, during what he thought of as an "interim" age. This was in line with St. Paul's earlier injunction to respect rulers who are serving God's purposes even without knowing God.[1]

Of course, this changed. After Emperor Constantine cast his lot with the church, what is now called "Constantinianism" incorporated a collapsing empire into a thriving church. Though at first welcomed by the church, it has become a matter of theological regret for many that the church became compromised by political and social power. Markus believes that the final Catholic repudiation of that Constantinian ideal came only in the 1960s, with Vatican II and the papacy of John XXIII. But for most of Western history there has been fruitful symbiosis between Christianity and the secular, involving politics, education, economics, science and the arts.

1. Robert A. Markus, *Christianity and the Secular* (Notre Dame: University of Notre Dame Press, 2006), 4-10. See Romans 13.

*   *   *

Secularization isn't a popular topic among either Christian or non-Christian scholars these days, and that requires some explaining. The prevailing scholarship in sociology, history, and religious studies tends to dismiss an older insistence on secularization in modern societies. It is a reaction against a time in the 1950s and 1960s when many social scientists declared that religion would rapidly disappear in modernizing cultures. Indeed, they took secularization to be a defining characteristic of the modern. But the West has reached its third millennium and the reach of Christianity is growing, not shrinking. Religion is a much more prominent theme in our news than it was in the 1950s. So in one of those swings of academic fashion, scholars are now more interested in counterintuitive studies of religious persistence, if not growth.While religious scholars may be happy to hear that secularization is going more slowly than expected, others have an objection to the very concept. They will insist that, if the whole of creation comes from the Hand of God, we cannot divide it into sacred and secular. If it is all God's, that must mean it is all sacred. If we had the eyes of faith we could see God's Providence in all things, so that dividing things into secular and sacred realms surrenders too much to unbelief.

There is a misunderstanding here. The objection mistakes the meaning of the terms "sacred" and "secular." In English and other languages that have grown up with Christianity, "sacred" does not just mean "part of God's creation." It means "things set apart." Set apart, that is, for the special purposes of worship and communion. Christians inherited this terminology from the ancient Hebrews, who had a healthy dread of the Ark of the Covenant and the sacrifices because of God's presence in them. A sense of certain things and times and places being specially marked out for purposes of worship survived into the usage of the church. But Jews and Christians also know that this sense of the special quality of such things can be carried too far. There can be a *superstitious* dread, an idolization of unworthy things. Nevertheless, they did not want to lose all sense that there are practices, times, and places in which worshipers are most likely to meet God. The sacred marks out passages between this world and another, where grace reaches through to humankind. Superstition can clog this area, and it seems to have no natural enemies; it can multiply and grow like a cancer that threatens a more truly spiritual and ethical understanding of religion.

*   *   *

It is precisely this fear of superstition that encourages us to recognize an area of the secular as a part of God's creation and plan. Even for believers, some of God's creation has no association with saving grace, but is there for our ordinary use. To think that all of creation is sacred would come close to pantheism, where everything is God. When everything is sacred, nothing is really sacred — which is a strain on full-time mystics. Christians more typically believe that we appreciate the sacred against the background of the ordinary — that is, the secular.

This goes far back with Jewish and Christian theologians. They have taught that by the act of creation, God made something *besides* Himself. The creation accounts suggest that we can use it with confidence, without fear. Western Bibles begin with a commission for humanity to take care of God's creation, not to bow down to it. This makes the job of theology easier, especially when natural disasters disturb creation. We shouldn't have to puzzle out what God means by every such event, but can concentrate on things that suggest a more obvious spiritual or ethical dimension.

Anthropologists tend to imagine that looking at "primitive" peoples living today is the same as peering back through history to the origins of all society and culture. Of course, today's primitives are twenty-first-century people too, and just as distant from our biological origins as we are. But we do notice that they characteristically don't make the sharp contrast between natural and supernatural realms that we do. They live in what some have called a "primitive fusion," where religion is about the real world and not just some spiritual realm. Anthropologists study many groups that don't have a word for religion and don't think of it as a separate part of life. Religion is not just part of their reflective solitude, but a part of their hunting and agricultural techniques, their cooking and tool-making, their social relationships, their reckoning of time, and other areas of life.

In time, however, anthropologists suppose that cultures sort things out. Religion becomes a separate part of life, and what is left becomes the secular. The secular area varies with cultures; there is no list of intrinsically secular things. Part of this process of intellectual differentiation is to conceive of gods and separate them from other manifestations of the divine. This enables societies to break out of a purely animistic view of things, by concentrating the divine and contrasting it with the ordinary. Later we suppose that religious *institutions* separate themselves from the other social practices of a people. So, ironically, separating religious doctrines and religious officials and institutions from other aspects of life is the first instance of secularization. Identifying the religious creates a secular world by default. It makes religion a matter of more conscious thought, and more open to doubt. While something may be lost in this process, other things are gained.

In another book I made a detailed survey of the changes to English life and thought in the sixteenth and seventeenth centuries, tracing how very many aspects of English society and culture began to lose their religious associations.[2] I discovered that my story was almost over by 1710. That is much earlier than historians had ever looked for secularization when they thought of it simply as the decline of religious belief. It became clear that the decline of religious belief was a second stage of the process, coming *after* the secularization of activities and institutions. There were even major religious revivals after the secularization of all these things: we think of the Victorian period, for example, as a high point of religion's presence in Britain, and considerably more pious than the previous century.

One of the most notable elements of my story was that the secularization of sixteenth- and seventeenth-century Britain was largely promoted by Protestant Christianity. In Britain's case the usual suspects as causes of secularization — urbanization, science, industrialization — came too late to be causing it. There, the primary causes were clearly the Tudor state's jealousy of the Catholic church, early Protestantism's objections to medieval religion or superstition, and printing presses that could spread the debate on these subjects.

Protestants were determined to tear apart the religious synthesis of power, belief, respect, celebration, and artistic effort that medieval Europe had built up. But why would they physically attack the cathedrals and their statues and stained glass, the roadside crosses, the monasteries and convents, the colorful celebrations, all the associations between religion and social welfare, education, justice, or political restraint? What Protestants said was that they were destroying idols and supersti-

2. C. John Sommerville, *The Secularization of Early Modern England: From Religious Culture to Religious Faith* (New York: Oxford University Press, 1992).

tion. Peasants who charmed their fields, or made the sign of the cross over each loaf of bread as they put it in the oven, or allowed sanctuary for murderers within certain churches, or named battleships after saints were making up religion as they went along. Protestants were trying to purify Christianity by scraping off these barnacles. They needed to redefine religion, to narrow the definition, to show Christianity's true essence and to spiritualize what had become mundane. For rather than elevating all areas of life, attempts at sacralization had dragged religion into the mud. Peasants were so busy with superstitious magical practices that they were ignoring the essentials.

Protestants tapped into a much older attitude here, which began in Judaism. Philosopher Henri Frankfort has explained how the creation stories of Genesis contrasted with the Mesopotamian myths that the Hebrews obviously knew, to picture a far more abstract nature which had no intrinsic divinity. Theologian Moshe Winefeld has shown how the further secularization of the Hebrew worldview can be detected in subtle differences between the two neighboring books of Leviticus and Deuteronomy. In Leviticus, there is still the same sense of the sanctity inhering in ritual practices and objects, attitudes that the Hebrews shared with their neighbors. In Deuteronomy there is a prevailing sense that the *intentions,* the *faith* of the worshipers, was the important element, rather than the things they used. The sacramental objects were more like tools.

New Testament Christianity had a Jewish background, certainly, but it was born into the religiously mixed situation created by Rome. Roman authority made religions compete in a marketplace, under the authority of the imperial state. While everyone had to acknowledge the divinity of the head of that state, they were free to follow their own cult as well. Jews, being intensely monotheistic, could not accept such an arrangement. They commonly assumed that it was Messiah's duty to overturn it, but Jesus apparently did not. At any rate, his followers concluded that they could live with the alien regime. Only if the authorities demanded that they worship the emperor *in addition* would Christians object, accepting martyrdom. They remembered Jesus as having prepared them for this, by saying things like "Render unto Caesar the things that are Caesar's, and unto God the things that are God's" (Mark 12:17), and "My kingdom is not of this world" (John 18:36). He announced a Kingdom of Heaven, which implied the existence of other kingdoms — secular ones.

So the church was born into a theocratic world, but it wasn't their theocracy. Indeed, the church's initial experience of theocracy created a bitter taste. In its better days, it has remembered this, even when the two institutions of church and state have maintained a wary alliance.

St. Paul honored the secular condition of imperial society in a different sense. We have the account of his visit to Athens (Acts 17:16-34), which became the classical instance of an acceptance of philosophical and religious debate. There he was taken to Mars Hill, just below the Acropolis, where people gathered to hear and consider new views. And there he adopted a style of argument quite different from what he used elsewhere. He universalized his message in wider philosophical terms. The days of conquering unbelievers were over; the days of debating them had begun.

Other religions have tended to grow up in conjunction with states, acting as the ideological arm of the regime. Christianity endured three centuries in which it lived under the shadow of state persecution. But three centuries into the church's history, Rome enlisted the church in its service. Nevertheless, the founding documents of the New Testament preserved the tradition of a Kingdom of Heaven that would never entirely be identified with any earthly regime.

Jesus made a point of the fact that power corrupts religion. Some historians like Edward Gibbon have complained of what poor citizens Christians were in a largely beneficent Roman state. We may take it that they were having trouble reconciling these two loyalties.

When the western Roman state began to collapse, around 410, St. Augustine wrote *City of God* to remind readers that God did not need a state in order to influence the world. This is how he understood Jesus' secularizing theology. The City of God would always be separate from the City of Man and could survive in it. Almost a century later a pope, Gelasius, is associated with the doctrine that clergy should obey the emperor in earthly matters, while emperors were to follow the clergy in spiritual ones. There was plenty of room for disagreement about what falls into which category, but just making the distinction recognized a secular sphere. In doing this, the pope was fending off a state that would have liked to incorporate the church within it, as happened to the Greek church in the Eastern Roman Empire. But all through the Western Middle Ages, the church and the various monarchies were separate. They often cooperated, but often they were bitterly at odds. The greatest work of

54

literature in that period, Dante's *Divine Comedy,* made a big issue of this need for separation. Dante didn't think rulers should be non-Christian, but he saw that they had a different role than churchmen.

*　　*　　*

Now we come to a big surprise: in the time of the Renaissance, kings asserted their divine right. We are so used to thinking of the Renaissance as proto-secular that we forget that divine right first appeared then, and was not a medieval idea. Medieval popes would not stand for kings trying to head up the churches in their realms. Rulers from Charlemagne on would have liked to be head of the church in their lands, but churchmen blocked that ambition throughout the Middle Ages. In England, it was the Renaissance regime of Henry VIII that established its jurisdiction over the church. And who was it that destroyed that divine-right philosophy? Not some secular party, but the super-Protestant Puritans. They resisted this totalitarian policy, and briefly set up a republic with wider religious toleration than England had ever seen. Here again we see a religious party promoting the secular distinction. The Puritans wanted the church to be true to itself, while denying the state any sanctity. (If this account seems unfamiliar, it is because of mistaken assumptions about churches and theocracy that we will examine in chapter eight.)

Theocracy is more of a temptation to states than to Christian churches. What state wouldn't want to enforce its ideology under the guise of supernatural truth? It is common nowadays to assume that the threat of religious "establishment" comes from the churches, but that misreads the First Amendment. When the Founding Fathers wrote the religious freedom clauses they were not outlawing the former colonial state churches, of which there were still several. Rather, they were forbidding the federal government from imposing a federal church over these state churches. They probably disapproved of the state churches too (Thomas Jefferson certainly did), but didn't feel they could outlaw them. Yet they wanted to keep their federal government from following suit. They didn't expect to forbid religious arguments from being used in political debates. How could one discuss justice or welfare without them?

Christians, of course, have not always kept in mind the value of the sacred/secular distinction described above. The separation of religious and secular is not a natural human intuition. We seem to crave the fusion of power and ideology, as in our ideological regimes today. What is surprising is that Christians founded the notion that power and its justification should be kept apart. They looked to religious revelation to make a principled distinction of religious and political power, creating respect for a secular realm.

Respecting secular political institutions does not mean prohibiting the use of religious arguments in advancing what someone thinks promotes the common good. If democracies call on public input, they must be ready to entertain religious arguments as well as secular ones. One of the sources of ideas of political freedom is that Christianity teaches that God respects the freedom of creatures. One shows Christian charity in the context of "secular" rules for decision-making that respect a similar freedom for others.

With its emphasis on saving faith, Christians should have trouble arguing that force would bring the Kingdom of Heaven to earth. So Christians must be able to live with — indeed, expect — secular politics. But they have often survived even under regimes captured by other religions, alien theocracies.

*   *   *

I will not spend much time on the ways in which Christians can accept and thrive in a secular educational environment. I discussed that at length in my earlier book on the secular university. I did not argue that religion should rule in the university, but only that it should not be ruled out. Religious voices need to be in conversation with others. Indeed, they were in such conversation from the very beginnings of the medieval university, when they engaged with pagan Greek philosophy and Jewish and Islamic scholarship.

The church's history of openness to secular elements in education goes back at least to the fourth century. When Christianity was accepted and even favored by the state, instead of insisting on an entirely religious curriculum in schools, Christian parents accepted the ordinary schools of rhetoric of their day. They knew that the texts studied would be the works of pagan poets, but they felt that to live in charity with others they would need to speak their language. Western civilization was born out of this synthesis of classical literature and Christian religion. In what we call the Dark Ages, the church would have been educationally poorer for having limited itself to Christian sources. And as is well known, pagan learning would have been lost to us entirely if it had not been for the monks who copied the ancient manuscripts. For all the older parchment and paper copies have perished.

*   *   *

A greater challenge for Christians is to deal with a secular social and economic system, by which I mean liberal capitalism. The relation between Christianity and capitalism is an illustration of how the two need each other. In chapter two we saw that capitalism is the secular form of economics *par excellence*. In its classic formulations, it does not welcome interference from other values like charity.

What we mean in calling theoretical capitalism secular is that it is a system in which money sets its own rules, without reference to human goals. It tends toward establishing as the goal of the economy not the good of the society but the good of money. Everything must be done to see that money creates more money, that capital finds its most fruitful use. Money ceases to be a means toward other ends.

Pure market capitalism insists that all the elements of production — land, labor, and capital — are entirely open to market forces. They should not be protected from the market even when labor stretches and sacrifices human lives, or when land use threatens our planet's ability to sustain our lives, or when money becomes subject to the deflationary potential of something like the gold standard. Humans cannot in fact live with pure market capitalism, which is why it doesn't really exist in any comprehensive sense. It must be regulated in order to be free, in Karl Polanyi's paradox.[3] For competition inevitably leads to monopoly — the death of competition.

The problem we face in trying to tame and manage capitalism is that we have abandoned any consistent rationale for regulating it. Its theoretical attractions shine through all our pragmatic tampering. We need something like respect for the human, or anti-trust fears, or benign monetary policy to protect *our* markets, those which serve us. So we create welfare capitalism, or relatively-free enterprise. But where do we find a

3. Karl Polanyi, *The Great Transformation: The Political and Economic Origins of Our Time* (Boston: Beacon, 1957, orig. 1944).

theoretical basis for our tampering that compares to the attractions of consistency in that secular condition?

There are, of course, theories of the Christian origins of capitalism. We may justify capitalist enterprise as the effort to satisfy people with goods that they desire. That would seem an exercise in charity. But what if there were ways to manipulate markets, to create the desires, to suit the investor? There are also theories of how some particularly Christian — specifically Protestant — virtues like thrift, anti-materialism, and conscientiousness became prominent in bringing capitalism to its position of dominance. These theories, associated with sociologist Max Weber, have been criticized from a number of angles, but may currently be seen operating in, for example, Central America, with the spread of Pentecostalism.

Yet there is a more impressive argument for Christianity's need for secular capitalism. Christianity apparently needed capitalism and the rise of the bourgeoisie to help break the power of *class* in Western societies. Capitalism became a great leveler of the old order.

Most of us would object to the view that humanity is naturally organized in classes, or that they are entitled to different shares of the world's goods. Yet this view was convincing to some of the world's greatest thinkers, like Plato and Aristotle. St. Paul planted the seeds of revolutionary thinking in European culture, but it took Christian teaching two millennia to help work the old prejudice out of our system. Egalitarianism is finally revolutionizing the world, and Christianity deserves some of the credit. But so does capitalism, which had its own motives for promoting equality. The presence of an aristocracy, which became parasitic after the state took over its police functions, and the presence of paupers, who were a drag on the economy, was fought by entrepreneurs in the name of equality. Christianity was unable, by itself, to break down class prejudice. It needed the help of capitalism.

So capitalism has shown its ability to work for good not just in improving the well-being of many, but even in breaking down class barriers. Yet for its intrinsic virtues, capitalism has a great many vices as well. It becomes a kind of economic terrorism when religious voices and others are told not to interfere in the public sphere. And it cannot correct itself when its leveling functions break down and it re-stratifies society.

In a similar way, religious voices could help in other areas in which secular forces have come up short. I have argued elsewhere that universities ought to counter the structural distortions of the news industry, and that high schools ought to counter our bottom-feeding entertainment industry.[4] But without a rationale that offers some view of human good, our institutions will not be up to tasks like these. In society and culture, as much as in politics and intellectual life, we need Christian and other voices to suggest the alternatives. When freedom simply means meeting the lowest denominator, or *creating* that denominator, it becomes increasingly repugnant.

We are beginning to witness a reaction to the sterility of capitalist society and culture in the new philanthropy, which has grown to staggering proportions.[5] It is a welcome sight indeed that those who have created or cornered so much of the world's wealth are now thinking about how much of it to return. But they may need help in thinking how that can best be done, and of what is valuable in and of itself. For they may well be among those who were in the habit of thinking of money as an end in itself.

*   *   *

Science is another venue for the symbiosis of Christianity and the secular. Historians now only rarely present this as a tale of "the warfare of science and religion," as they did at the time when secular universities were invented. The story they now tell has some surprising elements. The earlier science that the seventeenth-century pioneers of modern science rejected was a religious science. Religious, but not Christian. It was hermetic, astrological, alchemical, coming from pagan and magical sources. It is claimed that these sciences "were as much religious as worldly, as in alchemy with its techniques of purification and salvation, and their processes resemble rituals as much as they do laboratory experiments."[6] No wonder the church was nervous about them. The new cosmology that broke out of these worldviews grew out of a more Christian, or monotheistic, metaphysics. It was Christianity that inspired Ba-

---

4. C. John Sommerville, *The Decline of the Secular University* (New York: Oxford University Press, 2006), 139. See also below, chapter thirteen.

5. See *The Economist*, February 26, 2006, for an extended discussion.

6. Brian Vickers, ed., *Occult and Scientific Mentalities in the Renaissance* (Cambridge: Cambridge University Press, 1984), 32.

con, Kepler, Pascal, Boyle, Newton, and others to find a way out of this strange territory before other civilizations did.

What we lose when we adopt science as an all-embracing philosophy is guidance in how we should use the results of science. Western science is self-evidently better at solving many tasks than other intellectual disciplines. But it leaves to other forces the decisions about how it should be used, or what to study next. Religion, meanwhile, can often use the advice of this specialized knowledge to help with the goals it identifies. The two sides could respect their different functions. Confusing their different claims has been too common in both camps, as well as in our journalism and education.

*　　*　　*

Finally, we should mention the arts. There are artistic forms that are made for religion, which hardly seem at home in this world. One thinks of the hieratic art of Egyptian temples or Byzantine churches, for example. But Christianity often promotes an art that is rooted in this world. True, the ancient Hebrews were commanded to make no earthly image of God. But the book that contained that commandment as divine revelation is a book very much immersed in this world. The Christian Bible has sections at the beginning and the end that show things from God's perspective. In the middle it is immersed in human narratives, showing us failing and succeeding and learning. It is a history of struggling faith as much as mysterious judgment.

The fact that the West's sacred book is primarily narrative, and not mainly prophetic declaration, myth, proverb, "wisdom," or liturgy, has encouraged artists to use the figure of the human at the center of our art. The West tends to write novels rather than fables. Movies like Ingmar Bergman's *Winter Light* and *Private Confessions* show the divine interacting in a human context. Music like Benjamin Britten's *War Requiem* and Francis Poulenc's *Dialogues of the Carmelites* show that religious themes can still be brought down to earth in our highest musical expression. Jacob Epstein's and Ernst Barlach's religious sculptures show spiritual emanations in very human figures. This is all happening in a time we like to think of as secular, and when secular art is widely thought to be in crisis.

Christians have sometimes objected to the "worldliness" or secularity of art. There is certainly a point in demanding that art not sink to lowest-common-denominator entertainment. But most entertainment leaves you where it found you, whereas art pulls you into another place. The seriousness of serious art seems irreducibly religious. Most "worldly" art isn't nearly so worldly as it seems.

*   *   *

Christians are amphibious creatures. By that I don't just mean that they can coexist with a secular world. That is the approach of some Christian sects that try to keep to themselves, in a parallel world. Rather, I mean that one is *more* Christian for also being a participant in a secular world. A religion of faith is not shackled to others who don't share that faith. But that faith is supposed to engage the world in such a way that it may rub off on others.

Broadly speaking, we see the church's acceptance of a secular society in its willingness to accept converts. The history of Christian missions is full of the compromises the church has made with indigenous customs and concepts. There were times in the past when these missions tried to insist that converts master a standard Christian culture or else accept a second-class membership. But it has learned its mistake in this and has become enthusiastically evangelical. At its best, this implies a willingness to be inclusive rather than imperialistic. Imperialism was not something the church taught the world. It is something the church was supposed to teach the world to regard as sinful.

Christians shouldn't need to dominate the secular before they feel safe around it. When St. Paul debated Athenians at Mars Hill, he didn't threaten them. When Jesus' public teaching was through questions, he was assuming he had an ally in the conscience and intelligence of his audience. Even Christianity's opponents can see that spreading the gospel by fire and sword violates Christian charity.

Of course, accepting a secular realm or secular institutions need not mean indifference to unbelief. But many or most of the *things* around us are better seen as secular, in the sense that they are not part of our religion. Nor do I mean that in accepting a secular realm Christians accept a separation of public and private spheres. It is often said that religion belongs in a private sphere of beliefs or values, while science and politics form a public sphere of facts. But losing one's fear of secularity — properly defined — frees one to enter into "real life."

Christians should enter into the common arguments over truth and policy. There is no reason for thinking that their values are only matters of belief while secular ones are matters of fact. One of the mistakes of the old fact/value dichotomy was not to recognize that we cannot separate the two. The concept of fact is itself a value, depending on agreed standards. Everyone's ideas go down to matters of belief. It is true that the logic connecting ideas to beliefs is more solid with some people than with others. Christians should follow the lead of their best thinking in making their case. They must try to show that their answers are valid for others as well. Such an approach may not make others religious, but it can show them the point of religious faith and practices.

*   *   *

There was a time in the 1960s when a number of Christian thinkers in the "God Is Dead" movement thought that Christianity would actually realize its essential nature by becoming entirely secular. The church would entirely disappear into a society and culture and economy and politics that it had done much to create in the first place. They hoped that everyone would see that this had always been the tendency of Jesus' mission and message. Harvey Cox's best-selling book from that day, *The Secular City,* was a standard-bearer for the movement.[7]

And they had a point. They understood the history of Western civilization well enough to know the profound effect that Christian institutions had exercised on all aspects of life. It's the kind of thing one discovers when traveling to other civilizations and seeing important cultural differences.

But the 1960s would not be kind to the "God Is Dead" movement. Cox's book came out in 1965 — just before the sky fell on America. Our secular cities went up in flames, Vietnam and the counterculture pulled our secular campuses apart, and the optimism of the early years of the decade proved illusory. Many Americans found that traditional religion made more sense of the world around them than Cox's message did.

We would do better to go back to the thoughtful considerations of a generation earlier, which perceived America's cultural decline and looked

7. Harvey Cox, *The Secular City: Secularization and Urbanization in Theological Perspective* (New York: Macmillan, 1965).

for some better understanding of the relation of religion and the secular. The classic guide to that relationship was H. Richard Niebuhr's *Christ and Culture,* from 1951.[8] Niebuhr discussed five ways that the church had faced the surrounding culture over the years: antagonism, accommodation, synthesis, dualism, and a transformative or conversionist approach.

Fifty years later, the more natural expectation seems to be "tension" between religion and the secular. It is not simply Niebuhr's antagonism or dualism, because a church in tension at least expects to be part of "the world" and not reclusive. But neither is this tension simply Niebuhr's accommodation or synthesis, which would adopt secular understandings, as the secular theologians had suggested. It needs to be independent enough to be helpful.

Niebuhr's own preference was for something he termed a "transformation" or "conversion" of culture. He was hampered in describing this by not having clear examples of this in history, but found encouragement in the Gospel of John, St. Augustine, and other writings. Things have changed since then. Niebuhr was writing at the same time that the Jewish writer Will Herberg was describing the religion of America as a religiously-tinted Americanism. His *Protestant-Catholic-Jew* showed how great was the religious consensus of that time, so that one could then imagine it being steered in good directions. That consensus has now fallen victim to the "culture wars" that have characterized religion's interactions in the public square.

The most popular churches now tend to emphasize conversion of persons over changing of cultures. But churches are cultures in themselves, and could be models for the wider culture around them. To succeed, they need to know who they are, as we say, and be willing to stand for something. The tension I am suggesting will not be comfortable, but it might be helpful both within and without the church. The church's worst nightmare would be for Christianity to become merely popular, offering no challenge to culture, ready to be co-opted by everyone.

You may remember the story of Br'er Rabbit and his reverse psychology, when Br'er Fox threatened to fling him into the Briar Patch. Rabbit pretended his terror, but actually it was Rabbit's natural element. Maybe this is a good metaphor for the church. The church was born and bred in the secular world. It was born into a theocracy — but *someone else's* the-

---

8. H. Richard Niebuhr, *Christ and Culture* (New York: Harper and Row, 1951).

ocracy. It proved its transcendent nature by surviving and even flourishing in that environment. We may again be at such a moment, after many missteps when theocracy tempted the church. There are thorns in the briar patch, to be sure. But faith is made for difficult situations.

CHAPTER 5

Scholars Recover the Human Difference

W HEN I was a graduate student in the 1960s I wanted an overview of the history of philosophy and so I read what everyone read for that purpose then: Bertrand Russell's *History of Western Philosophy* (1945). Russell was himself a philosopher, mathematician, and spokesman for science. Religion had once made important contributions even to philosophy, he thought, but we needed to move on into the modern world.

Let me quote two sentences from the book that show where we were in those days. Russell begins his section on modern philosophy with these words: "Almost everything that distinguishes the modern world from earlier centuries is attributable to science." Then his chapter on Descartes begins, "Rene Descartes is usually considered the founder of modern philosophy, and I think rightly." The "modernity" he was talking about seemed rather unproblematic at that time.

Many readers are still at about that point sixty years later. Of course, it is common knowledge that one concept science has most trouble with is the human difference. Evolutionary biology has a sort of duty to find how much of what we think of as human is actually just natural, instinctual, materialistic, deterministic. That doesn't sound really human, in the sense of free, rational, moral, and so on. And while most scientists will admit that they are nowhere close to finishing such a project, some talk like it's only a matter of filling in details. They are the ones who get the attention of journalists.

Religion, on the other hand, has a huge stake in the concept of a human difference. If we cannot see ourselves as personal beings, there is no point in trying to see any kind of meaning or value anywhere. There would of course be no religion, which is the relation of conscious, moral beings to the source of their existence. But the point of this chapter is to see how intellectuals have struggled back to a grounding for belief in the uniqueness of our humanity, despite contrary tendencies of thought.

In the area of philosophy, Descartes helped to objectify humans by separating the ideal and the material and associating the human with the ideal realm. Since scholars don't accept the existence of that ideal realm anymore, his effort to establish a human difference does not inform contemporary discussion, in which we are led to expect that science will colonize all of knowledge. We should remember that Descartes (1596-1650) was a mathematician and scientist as well as a philosopher. And in the public imagination today, philosophy seems to mean bracing for the completion of something like scientific naturalism. As one philosopher puts it, "Cartesian dualism precipitates the crisis in the concept of the person, because it is impossible within its limits to think of *life*. . . . The identity of the person is a function of the identity of a living thing."[1]

The news from science may sound like steady progress toward "reducing" human concepts to lower levels of analysis, but in fact there are big problems involved. Some of the most notorious efforts to dissolve all human distinctiveness haven't been impressive. There was B. F. Skinner's behaviorism, and E. O. Wilson's sociobiology, and now Daniel Dennett's philosophy of "consciousness," which philosopher John Searle says reduces us to "zombies." But in criticizing them are we just relying on our *intuitions* of freedom and rationality? Are there real "philosophical" flaws in the materialist assumption? What alternative to scientism, naturalism, or physicalism do scholars recognize? Religion sees the human as an intriguing mystery, but are there more broadly accepted reasons to support that view? I will try to show that an answer to these questions lies largely in historical method and in language. It is the recent scholarship on language use, history, and narrative that most obviously establishes the human difference.

＊　　＊　　＊

1. Robert Spaemann, *Persons: The Difference Between "Someone" and "Something"* (New York: Oxford University Press, 2006), 136f.

The story I want to tell goes back to 1725, about a century after Descartes, with a book called *Principles of a New Science, Concerning the Nature of the Nations,* by Giambattista Vico, an Italian scholar (1668-1744). By "nations," he means human societies, so it is a science of humanity. (Bertrand Russell never mentioned Vico, who didn't fit his paradigm of philosophy and was still obscure.) In announcing a *new* science, Vico was attacking Descartes. Descartes' test of truth was our having clear and distinct ideas in philosophy, and a science based on facts and experience. He was holding out for objective knowledge, the kind everyone agrees on. He had no use for history or traditions in the search for truth, for that seemed like little more than mythology. One could argue that this makes him the father of the Enlightenment, the time when mankind was supposed to come of age and give up childish fables.

Vico argued that Descartes had all this backward. Objective knowledge was only knowledge of the outside of things, not their inner meaning. In Vico's view, understanding is limited to what humans have themselves created. We can't understand God's creation. We can understand science, of course, because we create science. But that is only knowledge *about* nature; it's not the understanding of nature that a creator might have, from the inside. We can achieve an intimate knowledge of what humans have built, of their art or literature, laws and cultures and history, because we are fellow humans. Descartes thought his ideas were clear and distinct only because he believed them, not because they were true.

So Vico's new science would be the study of the development of human societies, and he thought it would mainly encompass mythology, history, and languages. This is how to enter into the minds of ancient peoples. He thought this was the best way to understand humanity — not by introspection, as Descartes thought philosophical knowledge should develop. Our historical efforts will need to assume that people have always been using their brains, even when their thoughts aren't immediately clear and distinct to us. As we retrace their thinking, their myths will begin to make some sense, and their languages will show how they put the world together. We can go on then to study their ideas of law, of property, of class, of religion. The goal would be to come up with general principles that explain human development.

This is a very different approach than Descartes and Enlightenment thinkers like Voltaire and Thomas Jefferson took. The mind was the same everywhere, they supposed. People had just been misled, by their rulers and priests. So you couldn't learn from the past, except what to avoid. Vico pioneered the view that history is the way we learn about ourselves as humans, what it is to be human. The most profound question is not whether people's ideas in the past were true or false, but what they *meant*.

Incidentally, Vico was a very religious man, just as Descartes had been. Neither was a humanist in the sense of someone who believes that there is a set human nature that societies can build on. Or that the good in society must prove some goodness in us. Vico was like Blaise Pascal (1623-62), who believed that humanity was flawed from the outset. Pascal thought that the beginning of wisdom was in recognizing what he called our "wretchedness." Vico likewise thought humanity needed help. For him, God's providence must be at work when societies are able to develop in reasonable ways, and not simply by chance or by some natural principle of progress. But this was part of his theology, and not of his science.

*　　　*　　　*

Vico and Pascal were out of fashion and forgotten during the Enlightenment. That name, Enlightenment, has become ironic in universities nowadays, since it seems like a period of regression in some respects. It wasn't until the end of the 1700s that anything like Vico's insights were revived and attention was again focused on the human difference. This was part of the Romantic movement, which was partly an attack on the Enlightenment.

The name Romanticism may not sound very philosophical. It had to do with a search for holistic understandings of the world and for some vital, living principle in everything. In reference to persons, Romanticism was related to individualism, imagination, subjectivity, and emotion, rather than the Enlightenment's rational and objective "man." Romanticism is remembered for producing great poetry, and that grew out of a new view of language and how our minds work. It reopened questions considered closed by the Enlightenment, about creativity.

Among the leaders of this movement was Johann Gottfried von Herder (1744-1803) in Germany. He took issue with the Enlightenment view that language developed as a way to master our circumstances, and that it simply reflects a knowledge that precedes it. The idea that lan-

68

guage grows out of our prior knowledge may seem logical, but it's often wrong. Language may develop as a way of *expressing* ourselves rather than denoting things. Thus it often comes more out of our emotional life than as a way of solving problems. And language is not simply the result of conditioning. Herder stressed that languages are very different, and give cultures a different feel. They can induce new emotions, rather than simply reflecting prior knowledge. Poetry, for instance, can develop our humanity — our minds and feelings and judgment. So art doesn't just mirror nature; rather, it represents the artists and develops their insights. By these arguments, Romanticism took the focus off an inert nature and placed it on human creativity. Samuel Taylor Coleridge, the English poet, is famous for popularizing similar ideas.

On the subject of human societies, the Romantics agreed with Vico in rejecting Thomas Hobbes's view of human societies as artificial groupings that were deliberately created for the convenience of the individuals in them. We know this as "social contract theory." Romantics thought societies grew out of families and tribes that contained all ages and conditions, not just adult rational males. As individuals, we owe society a lot that we don't recognize until we visit other societies that seem strange. So it's not just individuals who are more interesting than the Enlightenment realized; societies are, too. Romantics considered the human realm much more absorbing than cosmology or chemistry, the big sciences during the Enlightenment.

At roughly the same time, a German theologian developed similar insights in reference to religion. Friedrich Schleiermacher (1768-1834) was concerned with interpreting the Bible. He objected to starting from the text and assuming that it could only have one meaning. He believed we need to start with the human authors. What were they experiencing, and how does the text reflect that? Can we retrace their thinking? Since Vico had been forgotten, Schleiermacher is often considered the founder of "hermeneutics," the science of interpretation. This approach makes texts of all sorts seem alive, representing a human truth and not Truth with a capital T, as science or philosophy might have imagined it.

*　　*　　*

So how does all this about myth and language relate to our theme of recovering a sense of the human? Sciences can teach many things about

Homo sapiens, about our bodies, brains, and behavior. But how do we learn about the things that enrich our experience, like our purposes, hopes, values, loves? You could poll people and create tables of the coded responses. But what we really want to know is what their ideas mean to them, so we can understand them. Their ideas are not just characteristics, like height or hair color, for persons are not just things. Understanding others shows that we are not alone, and confirms our intuitions of personality. A certain inter-subjectivity is justified when we share meanings in life. Social scientists, on the other hand, might conclude that people were not real and what was real was society. That is, *Homo sapiens* act in such predictable ways that one might not take their individuality seriously. After all, anthills are interesting in a way that individual ants are not.

In short, the study of language and myth begins to get at what makes us interesting as individuals and as societies. Language use and literature are creative expressions, which transcend what is instinctual or determined in our behavior. So we are not just the result of conditioning, and can't be entirely described in behaviorist terms.

Later in the nineteenth century all this became a little clearer to another German, Wilhelm Dilthey (1833-1911). He reproduced some of Vico's thinking, showing that the truths of natural science were different from the truths of the "human sciences." Natural science looks for factual relations, the objective outside of things. The humanities look for understandings, since we can explore other people's minds. (We can see this as the difference between neuroscience locating the energies involved in our thinking and our understanding how the thoughts seemed compelling to another mind.) So with Vico, Dilthey saw that we understand history when we can re-create the thinking of participants. History students of my generation became familiar with these ideas from British historian R. J. Collingwood's *The Idea of History* (1946).

*   *   *

At the beginning of the twentieth century, several thinkers returned to the theme of language as social rather than as an individual or a natural development. All the talk that English graduate students now hear about signs, signifiers, and the signified is about the fact that hearers are as important as speakers, and readers as important as authors, since there is always slippage between what someone means and others understand. There's nothing mechanical about communication.

The one thinker I'll mention from this group is Ludwig Wittgenstein (1889-1951), an Austrian engineer who became an English philosopher. With his technical background, Wittgenstein first argued the old view, that there could be a perfect language, a language of objective reality that reflected things. Bertrand Russell encouraged him in this project. But after writing a famous book in that vein, Wittgenstein had second thoughts and left famous lecture notes that proved the opposite, published as *Philosophical Investigations* (1953). Humans create the grammars which shape our universe and allow us to "know" it. By then quantum physics had shown that we couldn't really *understand* nature, but could only treat it mathematically and probabilistically. Nature isn't the model for our thought; our thinking is shaped by languages and how we use them.

What this means for our story is that human creativity came back into the picture — at the center of the picture. Languages are how we interface with reality, and they are "socially constructed." Wittgenstein emphasized this by calling our verbal efforts "language games."

But at the same time there were French thinkers, the structuralists, who went a different way with this. They thought that all languages seemed to share a *natural* grammar that shapes human thought. Languages show basic regularities across cultures that suggest that they are more a part of nature than culture. So the shape of our languages and thinking must reflect basic structures of our natural brains. Here, then, we have a naturalistic challenge to the idea of the human difference. A structuralist view of language edges toward "cognitive science," which is a natural, not a social, science, let alone a humanities subject.

Before the structuralists had gone very far with their project, however, they began to notice contrary evidence. Some of them became post-structuralists, such as Claude Lévi-Strauss (1908-) and Roland Barthes (1915-80). They and others like Jacques Derrida (1930-2004) showed how literary texts themselves "subvert" the structures they are supposed to mirror, as well as subverting authors' intentions. In this way our cultural products help free us from our natural condition. This was not the same argument that the Romantics had used, to honor the human genius, but it did qualify any simple materialism.

It was also clear that the post-structuralists personally exhibited a human difference in their moralistic enthusiasm for freeing humans from oppressive power relationships. It is difficult to make sense of an ethical interest like this from a purely naturalistic view of things. The most prominent in this sense was Michel Foucault, whom we will save for later.

Contemporary with the structuralists and post-structuralists, the study of language developed in a way that that jumbles our previous dichotomies. This was in the 1960s, when Noam Chomsky (1928-) founded modern linguistic theory by his critique of the behaviorist view. At first glance, it seems to threaten the human challenge to naturalism. Chomsky found a natural structural grammar in languages, but this was not something open to other species. Language is unique to humans, however it emerged. He insisted this was science, not hermeneutics, but that did not keep scientists from feeling threatened. They accused Chomsky of being anti-evolutionary in claiming that language must have appeared "overnight," and that it originated in self-expression rather than adaptive communication (and perhaps also for his insistence that language is unique to humans).

Our understanding of science as a human creation becomes important here. The *science* of linguistics did not arise unbidden, as language may have. Linguistic science is part of the great *human* project of discovering the secrets of the cosmos — we might even say the thoughts behind it. In any event, for Chomsky, language has the same relation to human life that our hydrocarbon structure does. They both underlie our thinking processes, as necessary but not sufficient causes. It is the ideas, purposes, goals, loves, values that constitute our difference from the rest of the natural world. The question of how the human could have emerged from its biological base is not as significant as the realization that it *did*. Indeed, the very use of the word "significant" illustrates a key human difference.

*   *   *

Perhaps the biggest name in twentieth-century philosophy, Martin Heidegger (1884-1976), raised the question of the human in an obscure but profound way. He was interested in showing how human being differs from other forms of "being" in the fact that humans *experience* time. Other things *persist* in time, but only humans are dominated by their sense of time, by their memories, hopes, dread. The most significant things about us are our awareness of our own deaths, of responsibility, anxiety, and all the other characteristics that show that we live primarily in the past and future. Heidegger, more than anyone else, showed that we cannot simply assume the self, as Descartes did. We must try to understand self in the "situation" in which we find ourselves. He inspired the later existentialists, and coined the term "deconstruction," which the postmodernists became so fond of.

A bit later, an American physicist, Thomas Kuhn (1922-96), dealt a blow to popular ideas about science. In *The Structure of Scientific Revolutions* (1962), he delved into the history of science to show that it was not what we might think. It wasn't simply the march of logical progress, registering true and important discoveries. Rather, the history of science was a very confused affair, involving mistakes, irrational proposals, ambitions, dead ends, treachery, and breakthroughs that had nothing to do with logic. Other civilizations have very different histories in this area. In other words, science is a fully human story.

Kuhn's special burden was to explain how scientific "revolutions" can happen, which require wholesale shifts from one set of assumptions to another. These can't be handled logically, since the shifts required to move from a dominant perspective to a "revolutionary" new one may involve different assumptions. Rather, such revolutions require what he calls "conversions."

Many scientists were unhappy with the popularization of Kuhn's theories, which often involved distortions that discredited the scientific process completely. But at least Kuhn reminded us that our scientific study of nature is not the same thing as nature itself. In fact, the scientific enterprise is proof that those who study nature shape and even transcend what they study. So in a sense, science might even be considered one of the humanities, as it tells us much about human goals and values.

*   *   *

The twentieth century also saw a recovery of narrative theories, something like a revival of the Renaissance shift from philosophical analysis to literary rhetoric. One of the structuring principles in language and consciousness that the structuralists noticed was narrative, with its insistence on thinking in terms of beginnings, middles, and ends. They objected to the idea that beginnings and ends separated life into separate stories falsified a reality that was more of an even flow. We remember that structuralists initially thought that such cultural categories are not as "real" as what we call "nature." The idea of stories implies actions and intentions, and thus stories assume a human or personal dimension as basic to the world. But Heidegger had stressed that our experience of time was the most obvious thing about us, making us different from the rest of creation. Narrative is the most obvious way of representing that, registering that we are subjects of knowledge and not just its objects. Our birth, life, and death represent the structure of narrative reality. Certainly those beginnings and ends are real enough.

The most prominent philosophical proponent of narrative, the French (Protestant) philosopher Paul Ricoeur (1913-2005), argued that narrative is an inescapable way of ordering experience. Narrative plotting reveals which events are more important than others, and is therefore a method of investigation as well as description. In the tradition of Dilthey, he reminded us that we can *understand* historically what we can't *explain* scientifically, just as science, on the other hand, "explains" things we can't understand. There is no danger of either one eliminating the other. Others have joined in the effort to show how the very current of existence has this narrative structure, quite aside from our descriptions of it.[2]

If narratives are real, then so is the moral element, for the very sense of an ending invites some sort of judgment on an episode, a point to the story. Critics as tough as Hayden White (1927-) can't avoid this realization. White protests that narrative and moral reality is "constituted" rather than "found," thinking that this makes it less real. But it's real if we can't wish it away once we've recognized it. When Bertrand Russell wrote his account of philosophy, he naturally made a narrative history out of it. He might have preferred to offer a logical diagram on the model of geometry, if he'd thought of it. But his history points to the human dimension in a way that his philosophy might not. Others have pointed out how the postmodernists' effort to overcome narrative and moralizing ends up becoming a narrative in itself.

Religious thinkers were quick to pick up on narrative as a humanizing perspective. Stanley Hauerwas (1940-) emphasizes how Judaism and Christianity have always taken narrative form, since their Bible is narrative and not primarily theological, discursive, or aphoristic. The Biblical writings and the communities that embody them constitute a narrative

---

2. David Carr, *Time, Narrative and History* (Bloomington: Indiana University Press, 1986), 16f.

which anchors a worldview and a coherent rationality. This realization has encouraged narrative theologians to see what happens when you treat Scripture as a whole, rather than making propositions out of it. This is quite a change from the previous two centuries, in which the Bible was analyzed to see if its truth was in the specific points. Within ethics also, a narrative approach has encouraged a new departure, emphasizing the narratives of character formation rather than the analysis of particular ethical situations.

*   *   *

With the mention of "postmodernism" you know that our story is drawing toward its end. I have spoken of post-structuralism and "deconstruction," which were important to it. While it was too diverse to summarize here, we may focus on one thinker who was its major prophet and deserves to close our survey. The French historian and philosopher Michel Foucault (1926-84) represents something like the moral of postmodernism's own narrative.

Until recently at least, Foucault was by far the most cited author by scholars in the humanities, despite the fact that his writings are purposefully scattered in their style and argumentation. Like a post-structuralist, Foucault wanted to subvert readers' expectations and make them aware of how they structure their worlds. So his books, which he calls discourses about discourse, undermine all particular discourses, all disciplines, all philosophies and sciences, and all humanisms, because all of these represent efforts to impose cultural power over some area of life. His intellectual histories resist a narrative or a logical character, in the name of an "archaeology of knowledge," in which one digs through the layers deposited by past cultures.

Foucault viewed everything supposedly human, including knowledge, as manifestations of power and desire. He broke down the distinctions of madness/sanity, coherence/incoherence, truth/error, in the manner of Nietzsche.[3] For the two of them, our assertions of what is natural or normal turn out to be power justifying itself. When you come

---

3. Our survey of scholars on the human difference need not involve Nietzsche, except to say that his view must be seen in light of his talk of the Superman. See Karl Jaspers, *Nietzsche and Christianity* (Chicago: Henry Regnery, 1961), 65.

down to it, Foucault considered all language to be an abuse, reducing reality to "knowledge" so that some elite can control it.

So what is left of the literatures and languages and knowledge in which we have tried to anchor the human difference? First, it is worth mentioning that Foucault never stopped writing books. He tried to avoid his own critique by a studied ambiguity and inconclusiveness. But there is no doubting his rhetorical power and wide scholarship, which kept scholars in thrall for decades.

Foucault seemed to want to do away with scholarship and philosophy as they have been practiced, rather than to send them in another direction. But what was the point of such an effort? Obviously, it was in the interests of the oppressed, the victims. Foucault seemed to long for the innocence of Eden, before what he called man's Fall into language. Indeed, he thought the emergence of the concept of "man" was the beginning of our de-humanization, or our alienation from nature.

In short, Foucault was part of a narrative of liberation. There is an irony in showing the truth about power by dissolving our concept of truth. But Christians could agree that Foucault has made a very forceful assessment of the human Fall, of the depravity of all human works. Christians have reacted in horror to Foucault, but he is in a biblical tradition when he denounces the idolizing of our creations.

So the bottom line is that the anger that seems to generate Foucault's irony shows his humanity. For our purposes, it is not so important that he agree with particular notions of evil and good as that his constant themes are oppression and freedom. Yet freedom, as his only unqualified good, doesn't seem adequate as an answer to our predicament. What would an absolute or total freedom look like? Freedom leads to choices, after all — and choices then limit our freedom. Christianity knows how to speak to this, as when the Epistle of James speaks of "the perfect *law* of liberty."

*   *   *

Religious thinkers might be able to raise new questions about humanity now that the human difference is easier to argue than in the heyday of Cartesian science and philosophy. While philosophical naturalism cannot justify a human difference, scientists can't help making exceptions of themselves as they creatively map out their projects. And secular philosophers should now recognize that historical scholarship, literature, and language use amply justify our intuitions of the human difference.

The interest we noted in narrative justifies a philosophical "personalism" that could be intellectually defended in the university today. Religious thinkers have taken the lead here. Philosopher Charles Taylor (1931-) recently explored these themes in a broad way in *Sources of the Self* (1989). Alasdair MacIntyre (1929-), Stanley Hauerwas, and others have shown how the church's spokesmen, as far back as Augustine and Aquinas, offer a philosophical grounding for the human difference. In fact, the concept of persons was first refined in the early church's discussions of the Trinity.[4] For "person" was defined in relation to God before it was used for the human condition. Trinitarianism allows us to think of the divine — of basic reality — as personal. For persons only exist in relation to other persons — dead and alive, imaginary and real, human and divine.

I don't think all this suggests a new Christian humanism. If we thought of humanism as an ideology built around fully-rounded models of human nature, that would prove constricting. It would suggest doctrines of human nature, empirically conceived, and a view of history that filled in our destiny. One might think something like humanism was justified by the Christian doctrine of the Incarnation, which imagines the divine finding a home within a human nature that is already in God's "image." But Christianity sees *finite* human life in terms of faith, which challenges human self-sufficiency. Christian believers pray for the *gifts* of faith, hope, and charity, after all. They don't consider them a natural birthright.

It may be impossible for any sane person to imagine not being human, in the sense of having no sense of self, purpose, meaning, or value. Certain intellectuals have tried to be consistent in rubbing out the line between us and the rest of nature. And yet the very purpose of such an enterprise, and their devotion to truth in this effort, argues against their project. For academically, as well as pragmatically, one cannot proceed without respecting our intuitions of purpose, value, and meaning.

Religion offers a dimension in which these human characteristics can be integrated. Many, even of the scholars I have mentioned, have found that it is in that dimension that the human finds greatest fulfilment. Religious thinking has a stake in arguments for the human difference — and ideas to contribute.

4. Spaemann, *Persons: The Difference Between "Someone" and "Something,"* 23-28.

PART II

Judging Religions, and Especially Christianity

CHAPTER 6

How We Judge Religions

NOW THAT the media are making us more aware of religions in our politics, our culture, and our foreign relations, we are faced with the issue of how we feel about them. Actually, how we judge them. We tend to be awkward on this subject and would like to avoid it. We were raised to ignore people's religious differences, and certainly not to criticize them. But we can't go on this way, just out of politeness. So we need a little help. We ought to be able to look to universities for wisdom and leadership on the subject. Indeed, who else would we trust for a task like this?

Before we even start on the subject of making judgments on religions, remember that religions have all had to work against the world's toughest, most resistant substance: human selfishness and greed. We don't need to suppose that the inhumanity that we find in our nature should be blamed on religion. There was a time when people thought that human nature was admirable, and we only needed to be freed of all restraints to let our native goodness bloom. This view had its best run after the time of Rousseau, when it blossomed in the ideology of Romanticism and the anarchism of philosophers like William Godwin. That lasted only until the time of Darwin and Freud a half-century later, when the very mundane character of humans was recognized in new ways. And shortly after that began the most murderous century in the world's history — at the beginning of a more secular age. It is hard to find anyone who still thinks that humans are little less than angelic. Many religions have taken a darker view of us, perhaps because they have been the main institutions that have tried to civilize us. They all recognize the strength of that selfishness they have to work against.

Having said that, it is still worrisome that religions may use their power to make people worse than they already are. This is what people mean by claiming, for example, that "all the world's worst wars were religious." Maybe you could have argued that before 1700. At least religions were part of the mix of motives then. But the world's worst wars, in terms of death and destruction, were those of the twentieth century, and nobody claims they were brought on by religion. To point out that chaplains were blessing troops on both sides is beside the point. We are talking about what caused the war in the first place, and recent wars have been caused by very secular ideologies — nationalism, imperialism, fascism, Nazism, communism. So if religion were marginalized, human evil would not stop.

All that is beside our main point, which will be that religions can only be judged by other religions. We'll get to that argument in a minute. It may be a hard idea to accept. We'll start with something simpler, which is that the first thing to be aware of is the difference between what people have *justified* by religion and what religion has actually *caused*. One could argue that it is when religions have wanted to be popular and fit in with the mood of the time that they have encouraged the evils characteristic of that age. It is obvious that people like to be encouraged to do what they already want to do, and religions are popular when they do that. But there have been times when people were genuinely led to do evil things, thinking they were being forced to it by their religion.

The accusation that religion is to blame for many of the world's problems, in the past and now, is a very common accusation these days, not least around universities. Professors don't argue the point so much as to assume or insinuate it. Students will learn to pick up the cues, and may sooner or later take it for granted that religion is not just useless but destructive.

There may be ambivalence in the discussion if there are students in class who object, and who sense that there are parents and donors and legislators who stand behind them. The culture still has a feeling that religion *ought* to be a good thing, and maybe even the focus of the good. This has resulted in the academic and journalistic assumption of the moral equivalency of religions and cultures. We tend to agree that there is enough blame to spread around that we can't pass moral judgment.

Since 9/11 it is probably impossible to maintain that position consistently. The cultural suspicion of religion has grown too large, in a world threatened by religious wars and civil wars. We don't know the history of the religions well enough to be confident of our judgments, and are nervous about teaching them directly. But there are thousands of bull-session discussions on the subject that would be better informed if the university gave the issue some attention.

*   *   *

One way to cope with our need to express judgment on this subject is to judge all religion to be bad in some way. One can point out inconsistencies or absurdities in particular religions easily enough. And one can always question whether they are really putting one in touch with the deeper levels of understanding and power that they witness to. We can easily raise doubts about whether they truly channel grace or only work on our feelings. But it is harder to *prove* that there is nothing behind religion in general, or that there cannot be a reality that stands behind our "ordinary" experience. How would one prove that, when proofs must be based on ordinary experience? Showing that religions weren't realistic wouldn't get at the problem, since religions question ordinary realism.

For a century at least, science has provided the most impressive answers to our questions. And there are sciences that attempt to "reduce" the concepts of religion to some more basic, more natural level of explanation. One thinks especially of psychology and sociology as having tried to explain religion — or explain it away. I have already argued that while they may show the mundane correlations of this or that particular religious idea or activity, they cannot dismiss the most basic sense that the religion is pointing toward.

In the absence of conclusive philosophical or scientific disproof, it has become all too common in academic circles to speak of religion as a disease. Without disproofs, we may fall back on considering religion pathological, a disease of the intellect or psyche. William James, a psychologist as well as philosopher, made this view respectable a century ago in his *The Varieties of Religious Experience* (1902). While he tried to go easy on religion, others have seized on his metaphors of "healthy" and "sick" to bring religion down to earth. These terms may justify a certain repugnance. A religion that people believe in too strongly — any "funda-

83

mentalism," for example — will seem "sick." But we may think it is only a severe case of what is always a questionable condition.

There is something curious about this approach, however. The very notion of disease turns out to be a religious concept, and not scientific at base. After all, there is nothing unnatural about what we call "diseases." Cancerous growths are as natural as we are, and if "natural" is what you go by, cancers have as great a "right" to exist as we do. Disease is like the category of "weed," which are any plants growing in the wrong place. "Nature" doesn't disapprove of them. The concepts of "sanity" or "health" or "disease" derive from our sense of the human good, and not from biochemistry. If we define sickness as "malfunction" we are pointing to some goal of our existence. And we don't mean simply passing on our genes, as sociobiology would have it. When we speak of the human good, we are getting into ideas of what life is for, of human purpose. These are in some fundamental sense religious questions. So when we speak of religions as being healthy or unhealthy, we are making something like a "religious" argument in judging religions.

*   *   *

I have argued that there doesn't seem to be a logical way to dismiss the whole analytical concept of religion, though we can of course object to particular religious ideas or activities. But how do we do this? All of the "world religions" are extremely diverse. So we will need to be specific as to which form of a particular faith we are criticizing. Objecting to Judaism in general, for example, would only show our ignorance, and we will be silenced as soon as we meet someone more knowledgeable on the subject. Then there is the problem that the varieties of the same religion will have regional variations of some importance. Judaism in Israel may differ from the Judaism existing in India, Ireland, South Africa, or Topeka.

Compounding this is the problem that each of these varieties has a history. Christianity was generally different in the third century from what it was in the ninth century, or the nineteenth, or in Uganda, Formosa, Alabama, Scotland, or El Salvador today. These complications will multiply the difficulty of pinning things down.

Then we might even take individual differences into consideration. It would be easier if everyone slavishly followed the official standards. It

84

is awkward to fault people for not following our best understanding of their religion. The same goes for accusations of hypocrisy. If we criticize others for not living up to their own professions, then we are presumably not faulting the religion but their personal failures.

If judging particular religions gets bogged down in details, you can see why we would prefer to criticize religion generally. Yet that is impossible; an analytical and nominal definition like we gave in chapter three presents too thin a target to hit. We must deal with religion as it is embodied in actions or ideas. We might think of limiting our criticism to Protestant Christianity, Sunni Islam, Reform Judaism, "Hinduism," Mormonism, Theravada Buddhism, or Unitarianism. But that proves to be hard, since even the members of those groups would have disagreements. It would only be showing how crude our approach was.

So the names we give religions are approximations. There is a striking example of this with reference simply to the figure of Jesus in America. Stephen Prothero's *American Jesus* shows how widely different are those who have expressed an allegiance to Jesus. He shows how dramatically this has changed over three centuries. The dominant images of Jesus tend to show a close relation to the gender stereotypes of the various periods, and to the national projects that have occupied us. It shows how multivalent our most successful symbols are, and how they may become cultural as much as religious in their significance.[1]

*   *   *

In attempting a criticism of religions, we must bring certain assumptions to the task. Readers of this book are likely to be in an American liberal-democratic tradition, which values freedom, tolerance, individualism, practicality, and respect for law. The students I taught found it odd that I singled these values out; what other values were there? This meant that they had never learned where their own traditions had come from. In fact, they had come from a Western Jewish and Christian ethical tradition, with additional contributions from Greek and Roman classicism. The classical values like honor and courage have faded faster than the religious ethics, however. They weakened with the wane of aristocratic

1. Stephen Prothero, *American Jesus: How the Son of God Became a National Icon* (New York: Farrar, Straus and Giroux, 2003).

85

class-consciousness in the nineteenth century. You might remember Nietzsche's despair at seeing bourgeois Christianity killing off an aristo-cratic culture.

With the classical virtues dying out in the wider culture of the West, Christianity will almost certainly be criticized on the basis of more or less Christian values. We don't recognize this if we don't realize there are other values, but assume that there is only one set which everybody honors to some degree. Conflicts with other worldviews and faiths are beginning to teach us how ignorant such an assumption is. It turns out that major religious traditions have very different basic orientations. Sociologist Max Weber spent much of his career describing how our great civilizations, with their very different outlooks on life, were built around the core of their religious traditions and symbols. And they have not lost those cores just because the religious beliefs have faded. The secularizing efforts of erstwhile communist regimes have shown how resistant those civilizations are to change. They still show vast differences between an orientation to charity, or to obedience, or serenity, or nation, or righteousness.

What all of this means is that our criticisms of Christianity are not likely to go very deep. When have you heard anyone criticize Christianity for being too loving, too charitable? It is criticized for not being generous or tolerant enough — just as Jesus would do.

The most common criticism of Christianity is hypocrisy, and as we said, this is actually a compliment. It is not a judgment on the religion but on individuals who do not live up to the teachings of their own supposed faith. The closest such a criticism comes to an attack on the faith itself is its questioning of the religion's ability to properly motivate those who profess it. Nevertheless, the standards of Christianity are the ones appealed to in such an attack. Of course, those religions have disappeared that were entirely too unrealistic or uninspiring to motivate their followers. But the accusation of hypocrisy means that the critic wants more of the faith, not less.

*   *   *

Given all this, some of the most obvious mistakes in judging religions can be easily dealt with. For example, there is the widespread notion that, after all, all religions worship the same God. There is nothing to support this claim except that many languages and traditions have words which tend to be translated as "god" in English. As for what they actually mean in those other languages, we are probably less clear. The fact is that not even all "Christians" worship the same God, if one could go by the images, ideas, and expectations by which they operate.

In any event, trinitarian theology makes Christianity unique among our major religions. It provokes major objections from Jews and Muslims, and also from Hindus, who have very different ideas of divinity. Those who have not learned trinitarian understandings may suppose it is an unaccountable idea which exists to generate a lot of tiresome and puzzling explanations. Those who are more theologically sophisticated will realize that trinitarianism is the *answer* to some very deep questions. It anchors the West's more elaborate notions of "personality," for instance.

The most troublesome mistake we could make in the matter of judging religions is to suppose there is a transcendent rational perspective that would let us judge between religions. This notion was a legacy from the European Enlightenment. More recently, postmodernism popularized the realization that there is no standard that could mediate all views — which had been the hope of Modernism. Instead there are various traditions of rationality or inquiry, as Alasdair MacIntyre calls them. Several different ones are sufficiently consistent and coherent to stand alone and make sense of a sufficient range of experience. None of them can claim to be simply "reason."

It is tempting to think that we should choose our beliefs on the basis of "reason" or "intelligence." Unfortunately, philosophical movements in the twentieth century have shown that intelligence is actually based on beliefs. Far from choosing our beliefs, we find that our beliefs have chosen and shaped us. Belief, after all, amounts to the assumptions, the pre-reflective commitments, that enable us to begin to think.

Science is no exception. There is nothing more basic to it than the assumption of nature's regularity. Science did not discover that, but began by assuming it. Otherwise scientists would never have worked so hard to find and describe that regularity.

Another assumption that was necessary before science could begin was that one could get true knowledge from studying only part of the whole. That is, we can find the "laws" of a *part* of a universe that is assumed to be pluralistic. In short, we do not have a *rational* science, but an *empirical* one, whose very basis has sometimes shifted. This has been acknowledged by philosophers as early on as E. A. Burtt's classic work *The Metaphysical Foundations of Modern Science* (1924). Whether you call your beliefs religious or not, they offer your basic orientation.

*   *   *

We all operate out of some faith, in the sense of our basic intellectual and personal orientation. That is the starting point for my argument that we can only judge a religion on the basis of another religion.

Our faiths are our basic terms of reference. So it is natural that they come into play in judging other faiths. This may not sound properly philosophical. But curiously, Pierre Hadot, in *Philosophy as a Way of Life* (1995), points out that in Greek times philosophies were something to *live* by, not something simply to *think* by. Logic, physics, and ethics were all supposed to be practiced as spiritual exercises. Philosophy was a love of wisdom, not simply a love of talking about wisdom. Philosophy was a way of being. This sense of philosophy was lost during the modern period, and especially when secularized universities professionalized the subject. But prominent philosophers like Wittgenstein and Foucault have recently tried to see philosophy in the old way again.

It may be shocking to think that our basic judgments somehow register something like a "faith." But religious assumptions are not always strange. Some look much more intuitive than secular ones would, and are almost too obvious to doubt.

Take the concept, or the assumption, of creation. Science has no real place for an idea of creation. Everything that exists or that happens points to something earlier that can be taken for its cause. Yet our government schools still expect students to see the wisdom in Jefferson's phrase, "We hold these truths to be self-evident, that all men are created equal." Students would be in trouble for arguing that we are self-evidently *not* equal. But if not created, in what sense equal? Can we say we have *evolved* equal?

Jefferson and his fellow Deists meant that people are morally equal, equal in rights or dignity. One cannot argue this within a naturalistic philosophy. Without the concept of creation, this thought would just dangle. The moral worth or dignity of persons seems to imply purpose in human life, and purpose seems to imply deliberate existence, or creation.

We are not about to give up the idea of the moral worth of persons just because it doesn't fit within naturalistic assumptions. Our "secular" schools move on, whatever contradictions are involved. Religious ideas are too pragmatically true to shake off.

As I have been saying, such ideas as health, wealth, justice, sanity, responsibility, and respect all imply optimal conditions of a "human" life. Health is not just longevity; wealth is not just money; justice is not just power. Trying to reduce them to these terms always leaves a remainder. But these terms and concepts won't go away, whatever our desire to be consistent.

So the difference between religious and scientific assumptions is not that the religious ones are bizarre. Currently, it is naturalism that is still too strange for anyone to live with, given our intuition of personality. Those who truly think that they are determined and robotic, without personality, are generally not taken seriously.

The new element in our religious landscape, and in our standards of judgment, is the Gnosticism of our New Age spiritualities. Gnostic groups were widespread in the Roman world, coloring several of the religions of that time, including some Christian groups. Gnosticism's ancient forms are sufficiently obscure that contemporary moral criticisms do not reach it, but Gnosticism has found sympathizers in the academy. It is often used to fault Christianity for its early and decisive opposition. And it serves as a useful foil in that it seems to have no negative implications, unlike other prominent religious traditions.

Earlier in this chapter, we mentioned that religions tend to be "realistic" in their assessment of human evils, but Gnosticism may be an exception. It held that humanity's true, spiritual nature was trapped in an alien, material body. The job of the tradition was to preserve forms of knowledge (gnosis) that could release one from bondage and let one's shining self ascend beyond a doomed world. This resonates with the current sense of a core of personal spirituality covered over by unwelcome social conventions (rather than the material limits that concerned the ancients). It may seem an oddly archaic viewpoint, but the fascination with Gnosticism shows how religions can be imaginatively resurrected — without their accompanying historical baggage — in order to ground our judgments on religions.

*   *   *

We cannot refrain from judging religious views or practices just because we think it is not polite. We do find reasons for our judgments, but we may not recognize them as religious in nature. We may not think we have a religion. If we are alert, however, we will find that our judgments reveal our ultimate concerns.

Our orienting perspective will not be religion pure and simple, for there is no such thing. Religions are not all cut from the same pattern, with only different names for the elements. Religions aren't necessarily even about the same thing. They probably do not truly understand each other. They have different notions of controlling forces, of human responsibilities, of blessed states, of beginnings and ends. They are entirely particular, and that fact calls for our tolerance. But if we are honest, we will not lose all powers of judgment.

Judgment of religions is something we are going to become more practiced at. For religions are not simply fading away, whatever secularization theory led us to expect. The practice of judging should make us all more conscious of our own basic orientation, our ultimate beliefs. Christian religion, in its classic formulations, teaches that we must respect the freedom of others in this area. It does not think that sharing our own faith, witnessing to our own experience, violates that respect. Indeed it would be intolerant to prohibit the sharing of one's faith. But when we do attempt to judge religions, we should be prepared to find our own views changing under their influence. We need to recognize that people with very different beliefs will view our judgments, our ways of life, with incredulity, disgust, and even horror. There is no reason, however, that we should not try to explain ourselves and even convert others to another way of thinking. Even secularists do this. It is not a form of assault — so long as we respect others' right to come to their own conclusions.

CHAPTER 7

How Does Christianity Come Out?

IT IS natural to criticize religions, since religions themselves include standards of judgment. I argued in the last chapter that any judgment on religions involves another religion, since they provide our terms of ultimate reference. This could mean judging our own religion to see if it has lived up to its own best lights. In this chapter we will try to see how a critique of our Western heritage itself would look, realizing that our own religious heritage must be involved, in the absence of any truly neutral or scientific standpoint.

There is widespread revulsion against the religious heritage of the West for the real or alleged crimes in its past. At one time the U.S. Supreme Court relied on such generalizations to justify rooting religion out of our public life.[1] The most common such complaints point, of course, to the crusades, the Inquisition, the religious wars of 1550-1650, persecution of witches, slavery, racism, oppression of women, anti-Semitism, or opposition to science. Beyond that, our lists may become more personal.

Various responses could be made to that list. An apologist for Christianity might try to show that these events were very different from our current perception of them. There is much to say along that line. The history of the Spanish Inquisition, for example, makes very dull reading if you were raised on anecdotal and sensationalized accounts. The usual small penances involved seem anticlimactic. The standard account esti-

1. See my *Religion in the National Agenda: What We Mean by Religious, Spiritual, Secular* (Waco: Baylor University Press, 2009), chapter four.

mates the number of victims at fewer than three persons per year, world-wide, over the course of its existence.[2] This pales in comparison to the actions of modern ideological regimes, and yet it retains its iconic status. One could make such qualifications of all of the issues listed above, which might tend to exonerate the church. But even if we were able to weigh the good that Christianity has produced against the bad, what would this prove? How positive would the result have to be to prove the truth, or the desirability, let alone the divine character, of Christianity? Would it have to be absolutely positive, or would the slightest tilt be enough?

Books like James Kennedy and Jerry Newcombe's *What If Jesus Had Never Been Born?* and Leland Ryken's *Worldly Saints: The Puritans As They Really Were* might demonstrate to some critics that Christianity was being judged unfairly. But that is only a defensive strategy, and only turns the edge of criticism. Even if Christianity was only the excuse for, but not the actual cause of those bad episodes, does that turn the argument in the church's favor?

There is another way to approach the issue. One might start by asking what our general reaction is to the list we just repeated. Why are we agreed that they are all deplorable? Who taught us to recognize these things as evil? Isn't it that they violate a religion of love? After all, Christianity itself teaches that they are wrong. It offers its own critique.

You might think there must be some other way of judging these crimes than a religious critique. You might suppose that there is some utilitarian standard that they violate, some drastic imbalance between pain and pleasure. Historians used to argue over whether the ultimate result of the crusades might be positive, in terms of increasing trade and prosperity, encouraging the intellectual exchanges that fed into the Renaissance, strengthening the European state-system, and so on. Perhaps they hoped this would free them from condemning the episode. The trouble is that such debates can never be concluded; one cannot isolate the variables, and the ripples from those events are still washing outward. One could never weigh the pleasure and pain of such events for any single individual, let alone a whole age or later ages.

So we're back to the condemnations from Christianity itself. No one

2. Henry Kamen, *The Spanish Inquisition: A Historical Revision* (New Haven: Yale University Press, 1997), 203.

is arguing that the Gospels or St. Paul taught war on unbelievers. The apostolic church taught submission to martyrdom, not crusading. Some of the later crusaders, like Richard the Lion-heart, were actually attracted to Islam, which related to the values of a warrior caste more easily than did Christianity. If one judged a religion by its foundational texts, the crusades would fail the Christian test.

Critics might imagine that ethics are somehow self-evident, and that calling our ethical standards Christian is a bit provincial. But in fact, ethics are relative to particular religions and ways of life. Other religions might not make the same moral judgments on crusading. That doesn't make moral judgments unreal; humans cannot avoid them. Furthermore, showing that people are criticizing Christianity on the basis of its own ethic is a way of ceasing to be defensive and going on the offense. If the most effective criticism is the hypocrisy of Christians, that can be taken as a commendation of the standards of the faith itself.

But that doesn't end the problem. For even if Christians learned crusading from the example of a more warlike religion, it is not exonerated. Why could it not resist temptation? How did it ignore its original sources? Few people have a bad word for an ethic of love, charity, individual responsibility, and respect for all, however inconvenient it might be in practice. But how did a religion with such a persuasive ethic go badly wrong sometimes? What forces in human life or in the religion itself could turn a religion of charity into something hateful and evil? This is something that should concern Christians.

Once again, there are answers from within Christianity itself. If I pressed you to think of the main critics of religion in world history, the name Jesus should come to mind. After all, the primary target of his criticism was not political or class oppression, but the way these things hid behind religion.

And how did he think religion had gone wrong? It would probably be true to say that he was angered that religion was used to establish the superiority of some people over others, to assert one's power or material advantage, or one's pride. In short, he objected to religion being used for ulterior and selfish purposes. Whenever religion became a means toward other ends than worship and trust, it turned the highest into the lowest. In the atrocities listed above we see Christianity being used for local pride, personal pride, class superiority, nationalism, wealth, and power.

Turn that around: when is religion at its best? Our heroes these days include especially those who face unpopularity, criticism, even persecution for the good, speaking truth to power. One's sincerity is not in question when one risks everything. (Again, Jesus comes to mind.) We can say this about whole religions as well as about individuals. So it is not all bad when Christianity is not popular.

Clearly it is best to keep religion separate from the institutions of power. Of course we are used to a legal separation of church and state. It seems the natural thing, but historically it is quite uncommon. Most major religions have grown up together with states, except for Christianity. It was born into a world where it was unpopular, when it was not allied with power, and it survived centuries of intermittent persecution before it was faced with the temptations of power and respect.

But the temptation is always for religion and power to go hand in hand. The natural course of things is for religion and power to be united. When religion is institutionally involved in all areas of life, the latter will tend to erode the more spiritual aspects of the religion. It would be nice if religion could drag power up to its level, but history indicates that this is not the way things work.

Jesus prepared his followers for this fact by his favorite metaphor — the Kingdom of Heaven. If we were hearing that phrase for the first time, what would we think it meant? The U.S. having a nuclear monopoly? The Moral Majority buying CBS? Osama bin Laden embracing a religion of love? Jesus' own images are very different — a mustard seed, leaven, a pearl. "My kingship is not of this world," he said; "the kingdom of God is within you." This prepared his early followers to live a life in opposition to present, earthly kingdoms, trying to obey God rather than the human powers.

St. Augustine made this point in *The City of God*. He wrote as the western Roman Empire was crumbling around him and Christians were bewildered. The empire had just made Christianity the one official religion of the state about thirty years earlier. How could God abandon such a perfect arrangement? Augustine took a walk through history to show that this was not unexpected. There had always been a City of God in the midst of a City of This World. Christianity did not promise that righteousness would rule in this life. Augustine taught that we get into trouble when we idealize our society or traditions. All states are based on power, and Rome was no different. Christians, he said, are like resident aliens or pilgrims. Though they must not abandon the world like hermits, they will live in permanent tension with the worldly City.

Even in the so-called Dark Ages the institutional separation of church and state preserved some of this realization. The church did not want to be absorbed into the state, and in its better days it maintained sufficient distance that it could be true to itself. The theory of the two swords, spiritual and temporal, was an acknowledgment of a secular sphere. Maybe the wrestling coach who taught history in your high school taught you that in the Middle Ages church and state were one, but actually, they were two. The emperor was not the head of the church. And that made Western civilization different from others, including Byzantine Christianity.

The church went wrong when it failed to respect a necessary distance from the secular and from power. We have seen earlier that Christianity acknowledges secular institutions, and may even aid those institutions, while observing the limits of each sphere. Jesus seemed to suggest that religion will find it more natural to be a critical than a creative force in society. The Kingdom of Heaven exists in the midst of other kingdoms, being a saving force within them. This encourages us to remember that Christianity exists in its teachings and should be judged on them, rather than on the institutions it creates. Few have a problem with those central teachings, of charity and mercy and hope.

If Christianity itself offers the critique of its own mistakes, we find that Christianity also offers the cure for its mistakes, in a recognition of different but interpenetrating realms. So Christians need not feel that their religion is threatened by criticisms of the church. Such criticisms are often Christian in their inspiration, and show how desperately the world needs its truths. If no one saw anything wrong in the church's record, that would truly mean that the world was lost. But so long as "the world" itself applies the church's values, even unconsciously, Christians may view it as reason for hope.

In all this, we should remember the point made in chapter three about how Christianity and the secular need each other. Christians should be the first to recognize that human power should be constrained by religious values without ever being equated with them. This is by no means a simple command, but it is at the heart of the difficulties we are thinking about.

*   *   *

Beyond all these considerations, we must observe that Christianity has been not only a critical force in history, but also a constructive, "civilizing" influence, with all the temptations to power that I have mentioned. How has that project gone? Has it been a force for good? We used to hear that it was. What is the evidence? Should we put it in the scale against all the bad that we acknowledge?

There are several general points to make first. When people justify Christianity by its effect on civilization, it means they are thinking of civilization as the overriding good. Christianity is being seen as a means toward an end, and presumably if we could promote civilization in some other way we wouldn't need Christianity. During World War II there were a number of books with titles like Reinhold Niebuhr's *Does Civilization Need Religion?* This raises the suspicion that religion is secondary and instrumental.

Second, there is not just one flavor of civilization. The very word is coming to seem old-fashioned, since we are increasingly aware of the failings of various civilizations and the dignity of "primitive" cultures. In any event, the world's most prominent civilizations have turned out very differently. I've mentioned that Max Weber became preoccupied with these differences and how they reflected religious roots. Civilizations think differently, from different assumptions and values, and this shows up in their arts, economies, social patterns, sense of self — their whole approach to life. It is safe to assume that Christianity has massively affected Western civilization.

Third, although civilizations are different, some criticisms have been leveled at civilizations across the board. For one thing, civilizations are accused of being socially oppressive, creating inequality. That's the Marxist critique. Civilizations overwhelm a primitive equality by their necessary class and occupational differentiation. For another thing, civilizations are accused of being psychologically repressive, creating widespread neurosis. That's the Freudian critique.

Both of these critiques are reasonably persuasive. They may have reached rather exaggerated heights in the 1960s, when some radicals tried "dropping out" to form communes that would escape such faults. But since then the reputations of both Marx and Freud have faded, both inside the academy and out. Psychoactive drugs are widely taken to be more "effective" than psychoanalysis, and the Soviet version of Marxism collapsed dramatically. Not that Marx or Freud were actually refuted. But fashions change in the academy just as they do everywhere else.

Of course, there were always limits to such general critiques. One can't just do away with civilization because it's burdensome. Still, we all understand that you can have too much of it. We understand the appeal of the simple, instinctual life — in theory anyway.

Christian scriptures could provide plenty of rhetoric against an over-civilized world. The flowers of the field are finer than Solomon in all his glory. Or, to paraphrase, lay not up for yourself stocks and bonds, where a market meltdown can make short work of them. The Genesis story of the ill-fated Tower of Babel has often served as a reminder that human ambitions can easily create insecurities and dysfunctions. If Jesus' teachings about social relations were taken literally, it would mean the end of concentrations of wealth or power. Then again, he didn't become a monk or hermit, like the Jewish Essenes of his own day, so Christians have generally felt justified in taking those sayings figuratively, if still seriously.

There has been one notable criticism of the church for not *supporting* civilization sufficiently. That was Edward Gibbon's *Decline and Fall of the Roman Empire,* published in the late eighteenth century, which blamed the church for shirking its social, military, and political duties. Gibbon notes that even after the empire became officially Christian, Christians refused to serve in its armies. They sneered at the philosophy and literature of the time. In his view, the peaceful, wise, and benevolent later empire deserved better than that.

More recently, however, criticisms of the church are from the other side. The church is criticized for encouraging the worst features of civilization: exploitation and repression, militarism, environmental degradation and rigid philosophies. These are all marks of civilization, though it's a civilization gone bad.

To sample a powerfully affecting critique of civilization generally, one might read Dee Brown's *Bury My Heart at Wounded Knee* (1970). It is the history of what happened when an advanced civilization involving white Christians met a primitive one, of Native Americans. The text is left in the heart-rending words of the Native Americans, who express their dismay at the utter immorality of the whites. The Native Americans were not paragons of virtue; their loyalty was only to their own tribes, and they didn't treat members of other tribes as having any humanity or

97

worth. But they did honor the promises they made to outsiders. They had only an honor ethic, with its self-regarding obsessions, but they were shocked to find that whites had less than that. Whites seemed to have utter disregard for the treaties they made, and may sometimes have made them in order to deceive.

As Native Americans saw it, white men's laws operated to ratify injustice. Their economy and credit institutions were organized to create inequality. They destroyed nature to create dependency. Their newspapers were used to spread falsehoods. Yet these were the things the whites were most proud of! They were the marks of civilization, along with their religion. If the white man's god was more powerful than theirs, it was also clear that he was evil.

In the book, the whites found reasons or excuses for their conduct within their religion itself. The Indians were heathen; their customs violated Victorian mores. The author is clear that religious missionaries were not the worst about all this. They often pleaded the Indians' cause. The uncouth frontiersmen also often got along well with them. The worst were the solid, respectable middle-class citizens at the center of society — businessmen and politicians.

Things go wrong when religion is used as a justification for what people have already decided to do. Sociologists have a distinction that would remind us of this: they distinguish between "culture religions" and "prophetic religions." A culture religion is one that is entirely implicated in the mores of a society, never presenting any challenge to its practices or values. Prophetic religions have some independence from the reigning culture, and may question the powers that be. Prophetic religions refuse to idealize their society, and may warn of its fallibility.

Prophets are not popular. They may be respected, but they are uncomfortable to be around. They may not always be right, either, but at least they aren't motivated by popularity. The challenge for the church, especially in times with relatively little persecution, has been to place itself more in a critical role than in a cultural one.

*   *   *

On the other hand, Christianity has been absolutely central to the formation of Western institutions that are now becoming the common property of all nations. Those who know little history may be surprised to hear of scholarship that shows how so many of the Western political, social, cultural, and even economic forms owe their existence to Christianity. There are several books worth mentioning in this vein. Scholars would not all agree on just how conclusive some of these books are, and the debates on these points may never be resolved. But the authors are not all writing from a Christian perspective, so their writings can hardly be discounted as Christian propaganda.

Christopher Dawson, in *Religion and the Rise of Western Culture* and many other works, shows how the medieval church was crucial to the establishment of *the stability and revival of culture,* after the catastrophic collapse of the Roman economic and political order. This included the *free cities* that were characteristic in the West, the chivalric tradition of *romance,* with its enormous importance for manners and literature, and the first invention of *universities* which combined research and teaching. Harold Berman, in *Law and Revolution* and *The Formations of the Western Legal Tradition,* has shown how ideas of the *restraint of power by law* grew out of the tension maintained by church and state throughout the Middle Ages. The idea of *constitutionalism* was one result. Ralph Barton Perry, in *Puritanism and Democracy,* is one of many authors who showed how the ideals and techniques of *democracy* were worked out among Protestant sects in America and Europe. Likewise, Michael Walzer, in *The Revolution of the Saints,* showed how *political radicalism,* the ability to form movements that could challenge tyrannical governments, was first managed by religious sects.

Max Weber, in *The Protestant Ethic and the Spirit of Capitalism,* argued that *capitalism* was given an advantage by Protestant ideas of religious calling or vocation. Because of its importance for understanding the great difference between the West and the rest of the world today, this thesis has been especially a matter of debate and revision, but its explanatory power has endured. Christopher Hill, in *Society and Puritanism in Pre-Revolutionary England,* developed Weber's idea of a *work ethic,* by which personal identity came to be bound up with one's job or profession, which is pursued for its own sake as much as for its rewards.

The effects of Christianity on Western culture extend beyond the pillars of democracy and capitalism. Along with several others, Herbert Butterfield, in *The Origins of Modern Science,* has shown how the roots of modern *science* can be found in Western monotheism, and in some of the attitudes toward work and nature that Weber discussed. In *The Secu larization of Early Modern England: From Religious Culture to Religious Faith,* I showed how *secularization* itself was as much the result of religious (particularly Protestant) ideas as it was of irreligious influences. Edmund Morgan, in *The Puritan Family,* showed how the conjugal, nuclear model of the *family* was promoted as an ideal within the West by religious groups. The list could go on and on.

As for judging the *value* of all these matters, that is a different thing. That is something that can never be concluded, since the effects of all these things will continue to unfold till the end of time. We can only assess them in terms of our present desires, fallible as we are.

*   *   *

If one were to judge civilizations on a Darwinian basis, by their survival value and success, at the moment it seems that the West has proved to be the fittest. That is not to say it is the best. And given Christian pessimism about human nature, it would not be surprising to hear Christians argue that Western civilization is committing suicide. Democratic egalitarianism may have invaded our cultural life to the point that it becomes absurd. And it is often suggested that the West's emphasis on individualism may be destructive of the social good, and even risk demographic extinction.

Christianity, however, may well survive the collapse of the civilization to which it contributed so much. We have now reached the point at which the majority of Christians in the world are not of European ancestry and were nurtured in other civilizations. And it is becoming clear that Christian religion is not limited to a single cultural expression. Clearly Christianity can transcend particular cultures. It may yet escape its long historical association with some of the worst aspects of Western civilization as its gospel moves into new associations with various worldviews. Indeed, it may be bigger than what we call civilization — and thus able to help bring civilizations together.

CHAPTER 8

Theocracy versus Christianity

O NE CAN hardly be unaware of the popular and journalistic concern over the dangers of religion in our politics. This is not just apparent during election campaigns anymore. With the rise of world terrorism, which seems primarily to represent religious divisions, it has become a constant theme. In our electoral politics, the accusation of being a "theocrat" would be fatal. Academics are obviously aware of these concerns. This is yet another way in which secularism feels that it is on the defensive these days.

It is possible that the growing concern with "theocracy" has less to do with a change in religion than a change in secularism. In our domestic politics the usual view is that the Republican Party has been influenced by resurgent religious fundamentalism since the late 1970s. But as historians have reconstructed the story, the Democratic Party, in the early 1970s, decided to change their party's appeal in a more secular direction.[1] Seeing the eruption of 1960s radicalism, party leaders decided that the future lay with college-educated, upper-income, and more secular liberals, and began to neglect their traditional base of Catholics, blue-collar workers, and Southern whites. It thus became, in effect, the first American party to take on a secularist coloration. As we will see in a chapter on the "culture wars," by the end of the 1970s voters on the right had become sufficiently alarmed and sufficiently organized to elect Rea-

1. Geoffrey Layman, *The Great Divide: Religious and Cultural Conflict in American Party Politics* (New York: Columbia University Press, 2001).

101

gan, who was the first to pay noticeable attention to his religious backers. This polarization of parties encouraged Americans to become more aware of a religiosity that had once been spread more broadly.

Journalists, if they leaned Democratic anyway, began to allude to "theocratic" leanings of those to their right. As Republican victories continued, such accusations became more frequent as they were found to be effective. It is now common to accuse conservative candidates and office-holders of plans to bring religion into American government. The journalistic reports may be hazy because of the ambiguity of the accusation. It is sometimes only hinted, in the way that the anti-Communist witch-hunts of the 1950s were conducted. Denials are taken as confirmation; lack of evidence proves how careful the scheming is. In this case, the mastermind is frequently identified as R. J. Rushdoony, a Presbyterian minister who served on native American reservations, and who died in 2001. His thought is given the name "Dominion Theology," though it is held very loosely by his scattered associates.[2] Locating a shadowy figure at the center of this web heightens a sense of conspiracy.

When it comes to specifics, the suspected goals may seem bizarre. After all, none of the acknowledged policies of the right would take us back before about 1960, minus the racial segregation. That was by no stretch a theocratic world. But the political and journalistic left needn't argue specifics if they can label the issues as "faith-based."

Those who raise the alarm about religion mixing in politics commonly take a different view when they reflect nostalgically on the civil rights movement, when black churches helped force the government's hand. What they agree with, they may not see as religious, but only as part of our common heritage — or as a cultural artifact of an oppressed minority.

Yet we know that there are indeed countries that are facing the issue of whether to establish religious law or religious governments: Islamist parties in many Muslim countries, Hindu nationalists in Sri Lanka, and the like. How about America? Are we in danger of instituting a theocracy, even through democratic means? What would such a thing even mean?

*   *   *

2. Bruce Barron, *Heaven on Earth?* (Grand Rapids: Zondervan, 1992).

To start with, we need to remember what the word "theocracy" means. It is the rule of God, which practically speaking means church or cult leaders taking personal charge, making themselves the focus of allegiance and decision, as in secular totalitarianism. This would be the end of political life in the sense of human deliberation. For such religious leaders would be speaking for God and would claim revelations that meant they could make up the rules as they went along. It would be the end of the rule of law.

This has been extremely rare in Western history. There have been many cults that have operated that way, as small enclaves within a society. But there haven't been many states or governments that acknowledge a theocracy. The most familiar instance within European history was the free city of Münster in Germany in 1535 under John of Leyden. Only he was allowed to interpret the Bible, so it always agreed with him. His government became a strange scene, but it did not last long. In fact it was the local Catholic bishop who led the forces against the regime and restored traditional institutions. Which raises the question of which side "religion" was on.

What is more common than theocracy is theonomy, which means the rule of divine law. In other words, the rulers are not a law unto themselves but hold themselves as well as others to a recognized religious code. The law should have a restraining influence on the leaders as well as on the masses. This is what Islamist parties aim for.

This also is extremely rare in Western states. The monk Savonarola's dominance of the city of Florence in 1495-98 was a theonomy. For a time it proved popular, but it was also ended by the Catholic church when the pope encouraged the political forces that were in opposition to it. John Calvin had some influence over the city-state of Geneva in the 1540s, but he did not interfere with the enforcement of the city's traditional law. Perhaps because Calvin was trained as a lawyer, he knew better than to try to institute some new religious code. Then, in the tiny wilderness colony of Massachusetts Bay, the clergy's political authority was even fainter. They could not hold political office, for example. After trying for a few years to enforce biblical laws, they fell back on English common law. So the famous witch trials were conducted according to common law procedures, in an older English tradition. In these cases, religious leaders or churches exercised influence over persons rather than power over institutions. By contrast, the recent Moral Majority never even reached as far as the Puritan divines. It tried to work with any leaders or voters who would support it on specific issues. When your hope is to create laws democratically, you are buying into democratic processes more generally, and it is hard to pretend that this is divine government and not human.

*   *   *

If theocracy and theonomy are hardly options today, we might consider what the union of church and state would entail. In such an arrangement, various church officials might hold office in government by virtue of their ecclesiastical office, as when bishops were chancellors or chief justices by right, running various aspects of the state and sitting in on governmental meetings. Monarchs might use the priests of the established church to preach in favor of their policies. But at least in Western history, attempts to bring the two institutions together often failed. Indeed, church and state were often rivals, and in fact this arrangement proved vital to the European establishment of the rule of law, as against the rule by a monarch's whim.

Christians in other parts of the world have had various relations to power. In the area once dominated by Eastern Orthodoxy, emperors sometimes held positions in the highest councils of the church, so that no papacy developed. Elsewhere, they might live under toleration granted by alien religions. In some places, such as Japan, they could be reduced to utter secrecy but survive for centuries. And in some Christian societies, dissident Christian groups might live in circumstances similar to those they might face in societies where Christianity was rejected altogether. So in the Christian tradition, there is no standard attitude toward politics.

*   *   *

We've already hinted at some differences between Christianity and other religions in this regard. I will discuss four: (1) the Christian attitude toward religious law, (2) Christian origins of church/state separation, (3) Christian origins of individualism, and (4) Christian church governance. My point will be to show how all these make theocracy very unlikely in contemporary Christian societies.

In the first place, Christianity is not a religion of laws in the way that some religions are. Christian teaching mentions law, but no major Christian group views divine law as what "saves" a person or brings the highest divine blessings. Law is primarily to reveal what the problem is, and that one needs saving. Divine law reveals the Creator's mind, or what God built into the world and into us. Christianity points out that it has become our second nature to be on the wrong side of these laws. Different Christian groups may understand law and mercy a little differently, but they all speak of God's initiative in reconciling humans to their original condition of trust. So one's salvation is principally by God's grace rather than by keeping or enforcing divine law.

This makes Christianity different from religions in which law has a more central function. In such religions, the human person or the society relates to God principally through law, rather than primarily through faith or trust. One can see how those religions might indeed think of substituting divine law for human politics. Almost no group of Christians would think that would save their country.

So how about those who want the Ten Commandments posted on schoolroom walls? At least in most cases, they are aiming at a more symbolic than legal statement. Several of those commandments are too subjective to enforce. Probably such persons just want some public acknowledgment that there is something beyond our normal laws, as our unofficial Pledge of Allegiance states that our nation and government exists "under God." They want it understood that there are absolute standards, and that national repentance is always in order. The same people are usually big on the Constitution too, and it would clearly be impossible to combine our Constitution with a regime run on Mosaic principles, by prophets and priests. So the current symbolism of the Ten Commandment is more in the line of America's civil religion than of Judaism or Christianity.

If anyone seriously wanted government to enforce the Ten Commandments, or any other Old Testament laws, they would run well afoul of Christian history. After all, separation of church and state was originally the church's idea. It wasn't forced on the church by secular politicians.

Remember how the church began under Roman rule. It was a persecuted sect, in the middle of a theocratic empire. Emperor worship was the glue that held all those peoples and all their religions together. Christians as well as Jews resisted this — and were unpopular for doing so.

They were called "atheists" for refusing to participate in the cultic practices demanded by the state. So Christianity always bore the imprint of being born into a theocratic world and positioning itself against it.

States have often invented religions, or used existing religions, as their ideological arm. And three centuries into the church's history, Roman emperors tried to do just that with the church. Constantine and his successors made it first a legal, and later the official, religion of the empire. But the church's founding documents preserved Jesus' imagery of a Kingdom of Heaven, so that there was no excuse for forgetting that one's primary allegiance was to a spiritual realm. I have also mentioned St. Augustine's influential work, *City of God,* and its point that God didn't need a state to influence the world. Around 495 Pope Gelasius I inspired the principle that clergy should obey the emperor in earthly matters, but in religious matters the emperor should let the clergy rule, which justified a secular sphere. In doing this, the pope was fending off emerging states that would like to have incorporated their churches within themselves.

As I have already mentioned, it wasn't until the Renaissance that the West saw efforts to unify church and state under the authority of Christian kings. This is Divine Right Monarchy. This is commonly thought to have been a medieval idea, but medieval popes would have scorned the idea that kings exercised absolute rights over the church. So it was renaissance monarchs like Henry VIII who claimed their own divine right, in defiance of popes. Uniting church and state was going to be the new thing, to get countries moving in more modern directions.

The Divine Right monarchs of the Renaissance didn't get away with it — not because of secularist arguments, but because religious parties stood up against them. The Puritans and other Calvinists were not willing to see this idolization of monarchs. So they resisted Elizabeth and the Stuart kings, sometimes at the risk of their lives, to keep religion separate from state power. Even when Puritans and their allies briefly took power in Britain, they secularized many elements of government that had always had associations with religion in earlier times.

This brings us to my third point: the individualism of the Protestant tradition. In the early years of the Reformation, Protestants were often in opposition to their governments, as the early Christian martyrs had been. Their resistance, in the name of religious sincerity or freedom, severely damaged authority in both state and church. They didn't really mean to do that, but after their struggles against those regimes, they could not re-establish the kind of social and political deference that had once been common. Religion, to Protestants, transcended the church as well as the state. In this way they ended up justifying an unprecedented individualism. Individuals were responsible for themselves before God, and not primarily through a church, much less through political allegiance.

At first, Protestants saw a vital place for the church and its authority. But circumstances made them begin to emphasize a more personal and individual understanding of Christianity. Faith, not law or liturgy, was the heart of religion, and faith implies freedom. Eventually they saw that religious freedom implies political freedom. God wanted free obedience. Since God doesn't force people, humans shouldn't, either.

This is the core idea of liberalism. Christians may now have a problem with modern liberalism, thinking it has gone too far into "license." That means that freedom is not being used in the interests of positive goals, but to indulge the ignoring of any such goals. Christians and secular liberals would agree that government should not force us to disobey conscience. Even if freedom is not used in the service of anything we could see as conscience, we owe each other the same freedoms we have.

Although it was Protestants who first blundered into this understanding, all Christian churches have since been touched by it. They have learned to see it as implicit in the accounts of Jesus' teaching. Toleration is now so ingrained in Americans that it seems self-evident, regardless of where it came from. But it is part of our religious heritage.

This brings us to our final point: how churches govern themselves. Are they naturally theocratic, or democratic, or bureaucratic, or something else? What are their deepest instincts in the matter of government — the ones they apply to governing themselves? Conspiracy theorists don't draw attention to the very disorganized state of American Christianity, which might undermine their ideas of a coordinated effort.

What we find in this country is that while churches have different governing structures, they all contain democratic elements. They are at least as democratic as America's political institutions. They may not have perfect democracy, but then democracy is a matter of degree, as is obvious when you think of how little input we have in our federal government.

In fact, religious institutions taught us how democracy works. Large-scale political democracies have to work out ways of letting us have any input whatsoever. The forms of representative democracy necessary to larger states were invented by Presbyterianism. The Presbyterian system of church government was the first kind of democracy that went beyond the direct democracy of the ancient Greek and Renaissance Italian city-states. It created a series of levels where representatives from lower levels would meet to decide things in the name of their constituents, with authority coming from the bottom up. This made it suitable for populations too large to meet together to decide everything.

Combining these points, you see that it is precisely our religious culture that won't allow religious leaders to seize control, except on the tiny scale of a local cult. The most notable recent totalitarian states have been secular, not Christian.

*   *   *

Having surveyed the institutional aspects of the theocratic accusation, we might still wonder whether there is an individual and personal aspect to consider. Is it theocratic to vote your religious views, or to introduce those views into political debate? Is that a violation of the separation of church and state?

Legally speaking, it doesn't matter what the *motive* behind your vote is. It doesn't matter what the *source* of your ideas is. It only matters what the *effect* of the resulting law would be. Does the law you helped pass force others to adopt some religion? Or does it prohibit a religion? If it does either of these things, it is a violation of the First Amendment.

Take as an example the issue of abortion. If the Supreme Court were to allow us to vote on the issues involved in the *Rowe v. Wade* decision, you could vote against it on religious grounds. But you might also vote against it on secular grounds. Some people think you could vote *for* it on religious grounds. But nobody at the polling station would ask you *why* you voted the way you did before deciding whether to count your ballot. The courts only look at the effects of a law to see whether it is meant to establish a religion, or to interfere with a religion.

So long as we vote, it isn't theocracy. Voting itself recognizes the rights of others to vote as well. God didn't cast a vote or a veto — so it can't be theocracy.

Then we have the issue of whether religious voices are using what is called "public reason" in making their arguments. A recent argument holds that on political issues we should speak in terms that everyone can understand, or not speak at all. That is on the principle that in democracies we ought to at least understand the laws under which we are governed. Secular ideas are assumed to be more "accessible" than religious ones, being shared or at least understood by everyone. Thus they have the potential to bind together our pluralistic societies. Religious voices are accused of making people feel excluded. Ironically, this argument is often used to exclude religious voices.

We can perhaps imagine religious arguments so outlandish that few would understand them, even among the religious community. But more people in America identify themselves as religious than as "secular," whatever they may mean by that. If you accept my view that the terms we use for human values or characteristics are ultimately religious in character, then you could not possibly carry on a political discussion without them.

As a crude example of a far-out religious argument, we might imagine someone promoting some economic reform on the basis that the New Testament suggests that we should have all goods in common (referring to Acts 2:44). Although such a socialistic claim would only have its full effect among those of a certain religious belief, it would be understood and might even attract others, some who probably didn't think they shared any views with Christians. So long as the effect of the measure did not *establish a religion,* voters could support it on the basis of their own rather different economic or ethical motives. There would probably be religious voters who would oppose it. But in any event, it wouldn't establish a religion and therefore shouldn't be a legally objectionable argument.

It is awkward to argue that religious people should be satisfied with secular reasons just because they understand them. They may feel they have outgrown them. They may think that religious views take more into account and offer a larger sense of what the universe demands of us. What we owe to others or to our environment may seem richer concepts in a religious perspective than in a secular one. To censor religious citizens because others are not in the mood to try to understand them would be undemocratic. If religious spokespersons aren't making sense, they are not going to be persuasive, even among the religious.

In 1986, Ireland, with its special constitutional relationship to the Roman Catholic Church, held a vote on the legality of divorce. The issue would never have come to a vote if the Roman Catholic Church truly controlled a theocratic state. The electorate had the final say, and the fact that their vote upheld a ban on divorce did not mean that the church ruled, but that a majority politically expressed the same position as the church. We talk loosely of churches being able to dictate to their adherents, but these are stereotypes that don't hold up well. It would be undemocratic for a secularist majority to silence religious views by exaggerated fears of theocracy.

PART III

Scholars Assess the Western Bible

CHAPTER 9

How the Bible Works:
Narrative Theory

A LOT OF people have wanted to improve the Bible. Not too long ago,
Reader's Digest offered an abridged edition. Thomas Jefferson cut
one up and pasted the parts he agreed with into a scrapbook. A lot of us
might sympathize, especially those of us who have set ourselves the task
of reading it from cover to cover. But how differently would things have
developed if the West's sacred book had taken a different form? And
what do secular scholars make of the text which is foundational to Western civilization and consciousness?

Humanly speaking, it might appear that the Christian scriptures are
the most successful in the world's history, if we can go by the number of adherents today. There are almost twice as many nominal "Christians" in the
world as the next religion, and to a large extent Christianity has spread
largely by evangelization. By contrast, the Quran is only available to those
who understand Arabic. Or that's what Muslims proclaim, by forbidding
its translation into other cultures. Maybe what we should be asking is why
the Bible has worked so well, given its somewhat ramshackle appearance.

On a subject which is so deceptively familiar, we need to begin by
taking inventory of our assumptions. If God had asked you what you
would need in the way of a sacred book, what would you have advised?
Students think in terms of textbooks. Shouldn't the Bible have been
closer to that model, for maximum effectiveness in getting some important information across?

Jesus was apparently literate; he could have written a book. Would
that have been the solution to improving the Bible? How would we have

treated a book entitled "The Truth, by Jesus of Nazareth"? One can see the suspicions gathering around such a claim. From our only records of Jesus' own treatment of scripture, it looks as if he thought that the Law and the Prophets were enough for his followers. So far as we know, he didn't even start on a book of his own.

*   *   *

I will begin by observing that the Bible is basically a large history. It has other elements mixed in, like songs, laws, proverbs, prophecies, letters, and visions. It is about God, of course. But it is much more about people. So it is largely narrative.

In the last half-century or so, scholars have become very interested in narrative. Historians and literary scholars had long taken narrative for granted. Like breathing, you didn't have to think about it. But just as breathing is pretty amazing when you think about it, so is narrative, apparently. There are many books on what is called narrative theory, having to do with literary criticism, history, philosophy, the social sciences. What is interesting about narrative is that scholars now see that it is actually an intellectual method. Much of the university still operates as if the only real intellectual method is analysis. Textbooks strive to be analytical, unless they're history texts. Analysis dominates science. We take things apart, by analysis, to study the parts and find out how they work. But now we are beginning to realize that there are subjects that are best studied by narrative, not analysis.

What subjects? Essentially, narrative is the only real way to talk about *persons.* You can analyze our bodies. But if you want to understand people, as actors and persons, narrative is the only useful approach. We haven't always known that. Throughout most of the twentieth century scholars favored analysis even in studying societies. Societies could be analyzed by structure and function. Scholars thought ethics should be studied by analyzing situations. They thought mind should be reduced to matter, because we think we know how to analyze matter.

But we now realize that all these approaches leave out the most essential thing about us, which is that we *experience time.* We *know* we exist. Other things *persist* in time, but they do not *experience* time. So analysis leaves out the most important dimension of our being.

Everything that differentiates us from the rest of nature goes back to

114

this experience of time. During the 1930s philosophers like Martin Heidegger realized this and began to explore ideas of Being that took our consciousness of time into consideration. The existentialists tried to explore those aspects of human being that were a result of our sense of existing in time — like death, responsibility, concern, freedom — which had eluded science.

Religious thinkers saw an opportunity here. Theologians like Karl Barth quit apologizing for the fact that Christian religion was in the form of stories. They stopped taking the Bible apart to fix it, and started looking at how it fit together and how that made it work. What is called "narrative theology" has made Christian intellectuals look more closely at the Bible's own organization and means of expression. This, of course, can hardly have been in the biblical authors' minds when they wrote.

As I noted in chapter five, the only thing humans can really understand are other humans. We understand humans from the inside, intuitively. Our own experience, in time, gives us the key to understanding others like us. We can only know *about* cheese, but have no sense of the inner meaning of cheese. But when we talk about understanding ourselves or others, what we really mean is that we can sense their purposes, plans, hopes, loves, goals. These are all things that unfold in time, by processes with which we are familiar. Meaningful discussion of these things has to take their narrative form into account.

Sciences used to try to study people from the outside, to attain objectivity. What scholars are now criticizing as "the Enlightenment project" was this determination to objectify everything, eliminating anything personal, and thinking that this was the very definition of knowledge. The "humanities," which had always studied humanity from the inside, came to seem old-fashioned and less rigorous. Scholars in those fields were too humanly involved to be objective. The point of objectivity was to gain universal agreement. Everyone would reach the same empirical results. Of course, it is true that we get our medical knowledge from that objective and empirical science, and there's no reason to stop that. But we've become aware that there's more to human life than that. Even doctors now understand that their patients' stories can be important to their cure, in a growing field that is being called narrative medicine.

Analysis takes things apart to understand the parts, assuming that the whole thing is the sum of those parts. But analysis doesn't work for anything that might die under dissection, or that can't be understood apart from its animating spark. Narrative studies the way things live and develop. And, to our surprise, it now appears that everything in the universe develops. The cosmos develops. Even what we call "matter" has developed, having precipitated from an earlier state.

These new views on narrative are beginning to penetrate the academy. There are some famously Christian ethical philosophers, like Alasdair MacIntyre, Stanley Hauerwas, and John Milbank, who have shown how narrative gives us a better approach to ethical theory. Ethics can be more fully understood as the study of character formation than as the analysis of situations. While rigor in analysis used to be the difference between the social sciences and history, social scientists are now beginning to use narrative methods in their studies. Meanwhile, history has given up its brief campaign of the 1960s to change into a social science by adopting analytical approaches and has once again embraced the virtues of narrative.

Perhaps the most surprising of these developments is that even science is beginning to understand itself through narrative. Of course, some sciences have always involved a time dimension, like cosmology, geology, evolutionary biology, and psychology. But I am talking here about the scientific project in general, the whole effort of unlocking the secrets of our universe. Historians of science now see that it could have taken a different course. The dots did not connect themselves, following their own logic or arranging themselves in schemas like the Periodic Table. Science unfolded historically according to the intentions of great thinkers and nameless ones. And historians of science are finally reconstructing the religious motives and assumptions that made modern Western science possible. For there are religious reasons that the West developed science while other religions have gone in different directions.[1]

Christianity has typically expressed itself in narratives more than in

---

1. See Lorraine Daston and Katherine Park, *Wonders and the Order of Nature, 1150-1750* (New York: Zone, 1998); John Polkinghorne, *Faith, Science and Understanding* (New Haven: Yale University Press, 2000); Martin Rudwick, "Senses of the Natural World and Senses of God: Another Look at the Historical Relation of Science and Religion," in *The Sciences and Theology in the Twentieth Century,* ed. A. R. Peacocke (London: Oriel, 1981), 241-461; John Brooke and Geoffrey Cantor, *Reconstructing Nature* (Edinburgh: T. & T. Clark, 1998); Mariano Artigas, *The Mind of the Universe: Understanding Science and Religion* (West Conshohoken, Penn.: Templeton Foundation, 2001).

analytical propositions. The Bible is what gave Western civilization its basically historical understanding of the world, which is finally penetrating our philosophy and scholarship. The sacred books of other civilizations may not be mainly human narratives. In the West, theology added the analytical element, with results that challenged its narrative character. But it may be doubted that theology has contributed much to the spiritual project of religion.

*   *   *

Narrative is not foundational only to philosophers or civilizations, however. It explains our psychology, resonating with those who have no particular interest in Jewish or Christian religion. Biblical stories are familiar, of course, being woven into our culture in a hundred ways. But stories more generally have a magical quality: the ability to pull you into the story. We tend to read our lives into familiar stories, so that they contain *our* story. Even if they are unpleasant, we find ourselves in their characters and understand ourselves within them.

This effect does not stop with individuals. Nations and ethnic groups find their identities in their stories. The Christian church is composed of those who find the most important parts of their own story in the Bible.

In other words, the Bible works because it sets our personal stories in a bigger context. The Bible would not be as engaging if it were only epigrams, rules, poetry, propositions, scientific laws, or philosophical proofs. Not only do we understand ourselves in its terms; we can actually extend the story so that it continues its life through us.

The fact that the Bible becomes our story explains why the Gospels are most Christians' favorite part. They relate to the person, the life, of Jesus, not just to his teachings. We relate to the other persons in his story as well. Scholars believe there were books simply made up of Jesus' sayings, like the hypothetical "Q." It is not far-fetched to believe that the reason these didn't become central and were eventually discarded is that they lacked the context that was necessary to understand it all. Jesus didn't just *have* a message; he *was* a message. Christians take his life to be the truth about God as well as the truth about us.

And of course, Jesus modeled the life of faith, in obedience to his mission, and the paradoxical triumph of that way of life. Jesus' life and teaching caused the most radical change in values ever. The world is still trying to absorb it, still trying to learn the lessons of charity. We can well believe that one must see that life lived out to understand or believe it. Such embodiment also helps artists to portray it, which may have been an advantage for Christianity over religions that are entirely transcendent, in the sense of being above narrative.

*   *   *

Recently, some narrative theologians have questioned whether we might not learn something from the way that the early church read their scriptures. Their way may have kept them from some of the difficulties that people nowadays have with the Bible. For the last two centuries, scholars assumed that the way to understand the Bible was to analyze it into its various genres and study each of these elements, the way a pathologist would treat a previously living body. But if we want the patient to resume its activities, if we want the Bible to come alive as a result of our study, one needs a different approach. Narrative theology looks at how the scriptures fit together or work together in a meaningful way. A little book called *The Last Word* (2005) by N. T. Wright sums up some of this recent work.[2]

Wright begins with an audacious generalization. He says that Judaism is all about the problem of evil. Jews were preoccupied with this problem because of their conviction that God was the Creator. If God was all-powerful, why did the creation "immediately" go wrong? And for the ancient Hebrews, a main issue was the suffering of their own people. If they were in a kind of covenant as God's servant people, why were they forever in bondage to one empire after another?

In Jesus' day, Gnosticism had an answer to this question. It was called Salvation. Gnostics thought evil only described the material world. Indeed, they thought that the material creation itself was evil, and that its creator was evil. There was a God above the creator, who was good but who did not interact with the material world. Men (and women?) could make contact with that God through their spiritual nature. Their souls could escape the malignant creation by the use of a saving knowledge. So in their view religion was about escaping the world.

Gnostics wanted to add books to the Christian canon that would

---

2. N. T. Wright, *The Last Word* (New York: HarperSanFrancisco, 2005).

embody this view of things. Church leaders held all this at arm's length. Although their lives were hard, they had not given up on the world. They weren't trying to escape a world that they thought was still God's field of activity. In fact the earliest church believed God was at work re-creating the world, and that they had a part to play in that.

In those earliest years, the church treasured a literature that few of us know, the accounts of the Christian martyrs. Reading them, one wonders why they would ever be popular. But to the early Christians, they told a more important story than just the pain inflicted on fellow believers. They were stories about conquering fear, and conquering hate, and conquering the flesh. And ultimately, they were about conquering the Roman Empire.

Jesus had shown the way. In their view, his resurrection represented a triumph over the power of empires. It similarly showed his triumph over the flesh, over fear, over human courts and punishments. In fact, the resurrection showed that the world was in the midst of a new burst of creative energy. Humanity was being born to a new life, and the church was the community of the new creation. This was a community not of power but of caring, bound together not by kinship but by charity.

A sign that history had entered a new age was the fact that the cross was no longer a symbol of the state's power over life and death. Crosses were now a symbol of God's triumph, and a sign of love.

Up till now, histories were of nations, but now the Roman world witnessed a new kind of community, a new kind of citizenship, of the weak, of outcasts and aliens. Christians were different, had higher moral standards, helped each other and even enemies. So of course the church attracted others, and they came from every nation, class, sex, color, and background. Potentially, everyone could join God's new covenant community. At a time when the Roman Empire had become too large for effective government, too loose and disorienting and individualistic to be supportive, the church was a new model of society.[3]

Of course, there was one other thing that the accounts of martyrdom may have done. They may have frightened off those who were attracted to the church for the wrong reasons. For those without real commitment, martyrdom was a warning.

3. See Rodney Stark, *The Rise of Christianity* (Princeton: Princeton University Press, 1996).

*   *   *

The histories of the martyrs were one way Christians thought about who they were and found their identity. But the bigger story was in the Bible as a whole. The early church thought of their scriptures (our Old Testament) as a universal history, still unfinished, in which they could play a part. But they continued to ask how God could be the all-powerful creator when injustice continued to triumph. Jesus talked constantly of the Kingdom of God. What kind of king was this, who could not control things? This was the question they saw the Bible addressing.

The early church began to see this universal history of God and humanity as falling into several stages or acts. First came Creation, when God brought something out of nothing, or brought order out of chaos. It's the same thing, really, since chaos is nothingness.

The second act was the Fall. God, with unimaginable skill, had created beings that had reason and freedom of their own, which made them in a sense godlike. Naturally, they could misuse those gifts, but God did not intend slaves or robots. But sure enough, the first recorded act of their freedom was to lose that freedom. Humanity fell into bondage to a desire to be gods in their own right, deciding for themselves what was good and evil. Stealing the fruit of that tree brought disorder into creation.

The third act was God's covenant with a particular nation. The idea was to reintroduce order though a people under God's special care. This wasn't necessarily a lucky thing for them. The main ordering principle at work here was the law that this nation was to live under. Thus, God chose not to re-impose order by force, which would violate the care taken in creating free creatures. The re-ordering principle, the law of the covenant, was an appeal to free obedience.

This idea of "law" was eventually broadened into the concepts of God's Word, the *logos* or divine reason, and was finally identified with the scriptures generally. But always the idea was that order would be restored through the reason and free action of persons. God would rule the creation through love. The law of the covenant and eventually the Word itself was the power that would restore order and heal creation.

But just as human freedom had not survived long, God's people showed that they weren't always up to the demands of the covenant. Their prophets never lost faith that God would somehow manage to fulfill the divine purposes that were part of the covenant. They never gave up all hope, even when the Jews fell into bondage to one empire after another — Egypt, Assyria, Babylonia, Rome.

Act four: Jesus. The Gospels do not hide the fact that Jesus' own followers were slow to realize how he fit into the world's story. But the resurrection, more than anything, proved that he had overcome Rome, as well as fulfilling the covenant and the law. So Jesus *was* the Word, and the Christ. His new life demonstrated the new creation. His obedience fulfilled the law in a way that the nation never had. Indeed, he transcended that law with his commandment of love, and modeled a new community in his treatment of women, aliens, seekers, sinners, and the sick.

So the Gospels and the other books of the New Testament were to show how the past had led up to a new creation and new covenant community. Narrative theologian Richard Hays has identified the covenant community and the new creation as two of the only three themes (along with the cross) that appear in every one of the New Testament books.[4]

The final or fifth stage is the church. This act gives equal billing to the church, the scriptures, and the Holy Spirit. They are in symbiosis. History would see this union decay, so that those called evangelicals are apt to assume that the Bible is sufficient alone, Pentecostals may think the same of the Spirit, and Catholics may view the institutional church as preeminent or even uniquely sufficient. But the early church knew how much it owed to the Bible. It offered the story that united different peoples, languages, and cultures.

* * *

In time the church lost its sense of being a movement. By 400 years after the birth of Christ, it was establishing itself politically and culturally, and this brought a change in the use it made of the Bible. Christians did not look to that narrative for the inspiration to survive. Rather it became something more like a textbook.

Through the Middle Ages and the Reformations of the 1500s, people looked to the Bible for explanations. Religion was becoming something to think *about,* rather than a way of thinking. They didn't *inhabit* the bib-

---

4. Richard B. Hays, *The Moral Vision of the New Testament* (New York: HarperSanFrancisco, 1996).

lical narratives so much as they *considered* them. And given that so much at the heart of reality is paradoxical, the scriptures didn't work as well as a textbook as they had as an inspiration.

Scholars began to direct the church into philosophy. This happened very early in the ancient world, in Alexandria, the cosmopolitan center of Hellenistic Egypt. Philo, the Jewish thinker, and Clement and Origen in the early 200s, are the important names here. To them philosophy meant Platonic and Stoic thought, concentrating on questions of "substance," that are of mainly historical interest now. In line with their training, they treated scriptural texts as propositions, to be reassembled in structures of their own creating.

Movements have a special feeling for their narrative. It was that sense of movement and mission that had formed the New Testament in the first place, maintaining a sense of the dawn of a new age. And in the twentieth century, theologians rediscovered the movement character of the church as it began to enter its current globalizing phase.

Connections between past and present began to emerge in new ways in the twentieth century. There were more Christian martyrs in the century just past than in all previous centuries combined. The church is more truly global than ever, now that missionary outposts have started to become indigenous communities. Competing ideologies are dissolving, reminiscent of the religions of the Roman Empire. So it is little wonder that we have a scholarly rediscovery of the mentality of the emerging church.

Recovering the narrative unity of scripture invites people today to see it as their own story. The scholarly and critical mode may warn against finding one's story in some larger metanarrative. But that view itself is part of a long scholarly narrative, and one that is as open to question as any metanarrative. The idea that we can opt out of any shared narrative is a possibility, but why should such opting out be a requirement for full membership in the educated public?

*   *   *

In a recent article, written by a graduating university student, the author considered how the gospel might strike her contemporaries. She observed that they were always suspicious of authoritative pronouncements, but they seem to have few defenses against narratives. They easily take too much from their entertainment culture. But in such circumstances, the gospel could be a liberating influence. The narratives of the world religions have elaborated their stories far beyond anything that our entertainment industry can offer. By now they are as resilient as our indestructible folk stories, and at least as rich with meaning. So our graduate did not think her peers knew how needy they were, or how unattractive their lives were, until they could see themselves in a comprehensive story of fall and redemption.

Americans are swamped with stories synthesized for our entertainment. They begin to cancel each other out, which is why we need new ones every day. The Bible is more like the enduring art of folklore, and the sophistication that comes when so many have had a hand in them. The scriptural canon wasn't all written at once. Even the New Testament waited a generation or two to come together, while different accounts circulated, and those that were most meaningful rose to the top.

Of course, I haven't talked about any supernatural qualities the Bible professes to have. That is something perhaps best found by experience. What I have emphasized is that the Bible is in the form that is truest to human life and our temporal consciousness. Narrative takes account of our attributes of purpose, desire, choice, guilt, and redemption, which unfold in that essential dimension of time. The church has apparently understood this intuitively. Science and scholarship are only beginning to come to terms with it.

CHAPTER 10

How the Bible Was Chosen and What Makes It One Book

S TUDENTS ARE fascinated by hearing that there are other sacred Christian books, not in the Bible. They are especially curious about the idea that somebody is suppressing them for some reason. Are we getting the whole story? Are we getting the true story? Is somebody trying to keep us in the dark, and if so, why? Bookstores carry titles like *The Lost Books of the Bible, The Gnostic Gospels,* and *The Forgotten Books of Eden,* "suppressed by the early Church Fathers, shrouded in silence for centuries. Now for the first time in paperback." There are loads of these in used bookstores, indicating that they didn't live up to expectations. For the fact is that they were never forgotten; they were just a disappointment after reading what *is* in our Bibles. That paperback turns out to be a photographic reprint of a nineteenth-century edition.

These books contain stories of the girlhood of Mary, how Jesus turned his playmates into goats, the further adventures of Joseph and Potiphar's wife, and such. People who have never read a tenth of the Bible may hope for blinding revelations in them. But only if you have always loved the book of Numbers would you get anything out of the Apocalypse of Enoch.

And yet these books are old, and some of what is in the Bible doesn't exactly grab us nowadays either. It's reasonable to wonder why some books are in and others out, which is the issue of the "canon" of scripture. This is a troublesome matter today because it has to do with religious or intellectual authority. Authority is a problem in modern societies that have embraced a sort of cultural democracy. In our populist and democratic environment, authority comes from polls or votes, where we don't have to explain ourselves. But we notice that those votes don't always seem conclusive.

The church is a different kind of community. It needs agreement rather than compulsion for the sake of peace. Throughout its history it has looked to the Bible as one basis for agreement, so the question of how the Bible was assembled is crucial.

You probably know something on the subject. The Bible is not just all the really old books of the Jews and Christians. It's not just all the books that talk about God, or all the books with helpful thoughts. You couldn't say it's all the books that God inspired, without having some criterion for deciding that.

Scholars have a very good idea how the canon was formed. It's not a mystery that some archaeological discovery will suddenly revolutionize. Jewish, Catholic, Protestant, and secular scholars are in substantial agreement on the subject. Unfortunately, there are many people who aren't scholars who are adding their less informed thoughts on the subject — and they get a lot of attention.

❖   ❖   ❖

It might be helpful to start with an analogy drawn from American history regarding the establishment of *political* authority in the United States. You will recall that at a certain point our basic document, the Constitution, was ratified by the states, providing our political scripture. You were taught that this was done by special conventions in each state, rather than by state governments. This was so the states could not claim to be the power behind the Constitution, and therefore able to withdraw their authorization later.

Actually, that story is a myth. It's a myth both in the sense of being a foundational narrative and in the sense of being untrue. What happened was that almost all of the states sent forward their approval of the Constitution *along with* a list of things that they wanted changed in the final draft. For instance, New York wanted over fifty changes of various kinds. But in the rush of business, none of those qualifications made it into the final draft. A few of them made it into the Bill of Rights. So in a real sense the Constitution was never ratified.

But nobody cares. The Constitution works. We had one breakdown when the Confederate states tried to pull out, and that was settled in a real cataclysm. But aside from that we are more or less satisfied with our Constitution. We only argue about what it was originally supposed to mean or what it *now* means, not whether it has any authority or not.

I'm not saying that, by analogy, no one cares whether the Bible is real. Only that establishing authority is tricky, like pulling oneself up by one's bootstraps. Really, we're asking the Bible to establish its own authority.

How would it do that? Some religions have a clearer idea how their basic authority was imposed — perhaps a prophet who spelled everything out from the beginning. But that would raise other problems that Christianity doesn't have to face. For instance, what if there was a Jewish council that decided the Old Testament canon or some Christian council that decided the New Testament canon? We might have objections to such an exercise of power. Who gave the councils such power?

The actual process, we will see, was quite different from that. Recognizing the Bible's authority was a very slow and cautious and generous and informal process, both among Jews and Christians. Deciding the canon was a process that involved the whole community and not just a few leaders. Many Christians believe there must have been inspiration involved in deciding on the right books, just as they believe there was in writing them in the first place.

Pope Benedict XVI, summing up a generation of the new narrative theology, notes that the scriptural canon has become more than the sum of its parts. He offers the idea that "inspiration" is not a quality of individual authors so much as of generations of readers who have seen meanings deeper than those the authors intended or recognized.[1] The same is doubtless true of literary canons as well, so that this becomes a more general scholarly concern.

*   *   *

To start with, the Hebrews had earlier books than those we have in the Bible. Some of the "Old Testament" books mention even earlier books that they were consulting. There was a "Book of the Covenant," mentioned in Exodus 24, for example. It is not clear that the Hebrews even had a concept of sacred books at that time. But books were very few, and

---

1. Joseph Ratzinger, *Jesus of Nazareth* (New York: Doubleday, 2007), xi-xxiv.

any book was considered to be deeply important. The Torah or Penta-teuch was apparently compiled over the course of several centuries, maybe 600 years, and in that time the idea of its sacredness did develop. Jewish scholarship, one of the world's most impressive cultural develop-ments, began with this consideration of which of their books were au-thoritative, and in what ways. They took a long time deciding. They weren't through deciding until after Jesus' time, although by then they had agreed on the ones that we now list. But we know that Jews of Jesus' day in Palestine (in the School of Jamnia) discussed Esther, Ecclesiastes, Song of Solomon, and Proverbs, which have nothing to say about God. What is interesting is that they left them all in their canon, rather than excluding them.

We see this same pattern in the early church. It tended to be more generous than some people thought they should be. It's not as if either Jews or Christians were trying to suppress something interesting. Chris-tian leaders wanted to hear from all branches of the worldwide church in settling on their list. They obviously weren't fanatics for consistency, or they would have eliminated the Epistle of James, for instance.

In the earliest years of the church its scripture was the Jewish scrip-tures, which Christians interpreted as pointing to Jesus as the promised messiah, the Christ. Those were the scriptures the church used in wor-ship services. And they did not tamper with the Jewish canon. They often took a fairly free interpretation of those books, by our way of thinking. Prophecy invites that kind of treatment, being allusive and metaphori-cal. But thirty-one of the thirty-nine books of the Old Testament are quoted somewhere in the New Testament.

However, in the third chapter of St. Paul's letter of 2 Corinthians, (probably written around AD 57), he refers to the Jewish scriptures as the Old Testament. For by that time the church felt they had to register a fur-ther revelation. Church leaders hadn't written much until that time. They hadn't felt pressed to do so because they still had the apostles as witnesses to Jesus' acts and teachings. But when it became clear that the apostles might die before the promised culmination of the ages, they be-gan to compile written Gospels. The four we have were not written in competition with each other, but for churches in different areas. Mean-while, by the decade of the 80s, collections of Paul's epistles were circu-lating among the churches. These didn't look much like scripture, being merely letters written to specific towns or to people now dead. But

Christians had began to see something profound in them, and 2 Peter 3 already speaks of Paul's writings as "scriptures."

The Gospels and Paul's letters were the core of a New Testament. The letters of 1 John and 1 Peter and the Acts of the Apostles were accepted without any problem that scholars know of. But there were others that were questionable: the other epistles of John and Peter, as well as "Hebrews," James, Jude, and "Revelation." The issue was whether they really were apostolic. They didn't have to be actually written down by an apostle, but they did need to embody an apostle's teaching. They needed that direct link to Jesus. Their apostolic connections might be debated, but we may assume that church leaders had more to go on than scholars do now. We will see that they thought it was pretty clear where to draw the lines.

As you probably know, all of these debatable books were *included* in the final list, rather than excluded. The point of the early lists of acceptable books was to identify which books could be read in public worship and teaching. There were other books that circulated in the early church that were considered suitable for private reading. These were unobjectionable works like 1 and 2 Clement, Barnabas, Didache, the Shepherd of Hermas, and the Apocalypse of Peter. These would have met the other criteria the church used, of being old, widespread (catholic), and orthodox, but not the crucial test of being apostolic. One might read them, but not for public worship — or as we would say, for teaching (that is, as a source of doctrine).

*　　*　　*

The churches soon began to experience a problem. In his epistle to the Colossians, Paul mentions an epistle he had written from Laodicea. It was soon lost, apparently, and two bogus letters appeared under that name. Church leaders spotted them as fakes. They realized that there were now books that pretended to be apostolic just to get a hearing for new ideas. Some of these promoted a religion so different that we have another name for it: Gnosticism.

This is where the Gospel of Thomas comes in. It has caused great excitement since it was recovered in 1946 in Egypt. Actually there is more than one Gospel of Thomas, and also Gospels of Peter, James, Bartholomew, and Matthias, as well as Acts of Andrew, Paul, Philip, and

128

John, among others. Many of these included elements of Gnosticism. Gnostics might differ among themselves, but in general they tended to believe that Jesus had never really been human and had not died. So their historical sense was entirely different from the church's. The riddles in these Gnostic Gospels offered the secret, saving knowledge which was the heart of that system. Nothing could be further from Christianity, which wanted the gospel, the Good News, to be as public and as clear as possible. They preached that God wills the salvation of all humanity and has already provided for their redemption.

The early church outlasted these sects. It couldn't suppress them, because this was before the church was even legal and lacked the power of the state behind it. Yet the sects disappeared so thoroughly that the Gospel of Thomas was long known only through the Christian refutations of it. It did not inspire enduring religious communities, being so intensely individualistic.

When people nowadays hear of these other Gospels, they may think that room should be made for them in the canon. They think they might contain some authentic traditions from Jesus' time. And of course they might. But that is not the only criterion of what Christians mean by scripture. The Gospel of Thomas is the one that seems most likely to contain some such authentic traditions. But anyone familiar with the canonical books will find much of it simply unacceptable — not least, for example, when it discusses the fact that women don't have souls.

*   *   *

Scholarly efforts to go beyond the canonical Gospels to retrieve the real story are in the tradition of the so-called Quest for the Historical Jesus. This is the name given to the nineteenth-century effort to write a scholarly account of Jesus' life. By about 1910 scholars like Albert Schweitzer concluded that such a quest is not possible. Archaeology and related fields will never get closer than the church's own traditions. Of course, anyone is free to doubt the truth of parts of the canonical Gospels. But we would just be guessing what to accept from the extra-canonical writings. People who want actual religious guidance for their lives are not going to be impressed with someone's scholarly guesses.

The pseudepigrapha, or pseudonymous writings, are genuinely old, however, and can tell us much about the world in which Christianity was born and in which it succeeded. That is their value. What they can't tell us is reliable information about Jesus or what the main body of Jesus' followers thought about him.

The church may have rejected the heretics' contributions, but it learned from them as well. For instance, one named Marcion was the first to create a New Testament, about AD 150, which he did by excluding all the Gospels except Luke and all the rest of the New Testament except ten of Paul's epistles. This strictly Gentile canon seems to have caused the church to react by being more inclusive. Another named Tatian created a harmonization of the four canonical Gospels, called the *Diatessaron*, about 170. In reaction, the church learned to appreciate the advantages of keeping all four, despite the differences among them that they were well aware of. And even Tatian knew to leave out the Gnostic Gospels.

*   *   *

So a consideration of the canon went on for several centuries, many generations. It was slowed by a number of factors. The church was spread all around the empire; it was still illegal and had difficulty communicating; and it operated in the different languages of Greek, Syriac, Latin, and Coptic. Because it had no one headquarters, leaders wanted to hear from all the corners of the church. There were common criteria: everyone went by apostolic associations, but they also factored in the experience of churches in using books in teaching and worship. Things written with the obvious intention of changing the apostolic message were rejected.

Finally, by 367 we know there was an encyclical of Athanasius in the Eastern church that set out the list we have. Then there were councils in the West — actually North Africa (Hippo in 393 and Carthage in 397) — that agreed. They didn't decree this canon, but only observed that this was the church's practice. Notice that no church council ever commissioned new books or even announced the criteria for the canon, which seemed self-evident. But the list they agreed on constitutes the New Testament canon of the church today, whether Catholic, Protestant, or Orthodox.

Some historians would say that the church created scripture; others might say that scripture created the church. Both views make some sense. Certainly we can agree that having this authoritative apostolic/scriptural basis gave the church its advantage in a wide-open religious situation. This was a time when the empires of Alexander and of Rome had made people aware of the many religions of the known world. Converts entered the church wanting to bring some of their favorite ideas in with them. The canon helped Christians to insist on a simple, public faith.

Finally, saying that the early church made decisions with regard to scripture does not mean that the church now feels free to keep changing it to keep things up-to-date. Living persons constitute the church's present members, but it wants to respect those of the past as well. There were perhaps eight or ten generations involved in identifying the canon, and we are far more remote from the apostles. We can *interpret* scripture anew, of course, which deepens the canon. But the church tries to acknowledge those who lived through trials in its history. This is a way of showing that the church is not making things up to suit itself.

*   *   *

Now the question becomes, what makes the Bible one book and not many? And is multiple authorship an advantage in any way? It certainly seems a shaky way to settle authority within a religion. It raises the possibilities of incoherence or contradiction. Paul Ricoeur, the prominent French philosopher, takes the view that the *closing* of the biblical canon, an unheralded event, was of highest significance in determining the relations of all the parts and genres included within it. In his view, those who have tried to explode the canon by relating the genres to modernist analysis risk losing its sense entirely.[2] And more scholars now, under the influence of narrative theories, are in the mood to consider the powerful unity that it seems to possess.

In Greek, *biblia* means books in the plural. We are all aware that it is a collection of books written over the course of many centuries. More than a thousand years, in fact. More than a thousand years *ago* would put us back into the 900s. That is a very different, almost legendary world. People's minds were different then. How much coherence would a book written over the course of a thousand years have? And do other religions' sacred books escape this problem?

2. Paul Ricoeur, *Figuring the Sacred: Religion, Narrative, and Imagination*, ed. Mark I. Wallace (Minneapolis: Fortress, 1995), 41.

Of course, I'm talking about the differences between Old and New Testaments, between Jewish and Christian authors, between Hebrew and Greek concepts, between Jesus and Paul, Paul and James, priestly versus prophetic, courtly versus prophetic. There are notable tensions, paradoxes, contradictions — law versus faith, blood sacrifice versus grace, warlike and pacifist, judgment and love, nationalistic and universalistic. All this seems like a weakness. We need to look at how the assembly of books that make up the Christian Bible would look to other traditions: Jews, Muslims, and secular scholars.

*   *   *

There has been a temptation at times for Christians to ignore the Old Testament, to escape embarrassing things in it. It often doesn't seem to contain a religion of love and universal brotherhood. Western missionaries to India and China have sometimes discussed whether they should mention the Old Testament at all, for fear of discrediting Christianity. Some of them have thought it would be more effective to show how the local religions were themselves a similar preparation for Christianity. Instead of using the Old Testament as a preparation for Jesus, they would take concepts their audience is familiar with and show how Christianity completes them.

Yet on this topic an Anglican bishop in India, Lesslie Newbigin, quotes a Hindu friend of his, who said, "As I read your Bible I find in it a quite unique interpretation of universal history and, therefore, a unique understanding of the human person as a responsible actor in history. You Christian missionaries have talked of the Bible as [if] it were simply another book of religion. We have plenty of these already in India."[3] What did that man see in the Bible that we may not be noticing?

Some scholars reject any concept of an overall message in the Bible. Would they be more receptive to a sacred text that was produced something like the Quran? The Quran was written over a very short period (Mohammed lived maybe 570-632), in just a couple of consistent voices, and laying down law in no uncertain terms. It actually announces that it is inspired, which few of the biblical books do.

But the Quran does have a problem. It is actually only half a book.

3. Lesslie Newbigin, *The Gospel in a Pluralist Society* (Grand Rapids: Eerdmans, 1989), 89.

That is because it was built on top of the Bible, which Mohammed knew something about. He used words and concepts and doctrines that he had picked up from Jews and Christians. He even mentions the Old and New Testaments.

Muslims claim that Mohammed was illiterate. We may think of that as an admission of something they would rather have concealed, but actually it could be seen as a boast. They are claiming that Mohammed could not have been influenced by things he had read. Therefore we can trust his revelations as something straight from God, and not what he derived from influences around him. The authority of the Quran, they say, is in the "inimitable" poetry of its expression. That is, it can't be imitated, being beyond human possibility. It follows that one should not translate the Quran out of Arabic for fear of losing the poetry which establishes that authority. Jews and Christians do not make such stylistic claims for their sacred books, and are eager to translate them into other cultures.

The Quran uses some complicated ideas like creation, covenant, law, atonement, election, faith, and sacrament. These concepts are not self-evident; we're not born with them. They developed over a very long period of time. And that is one of the interesting things about the Bible; it contains much of that development. The Quran can simply assume it. The Quran also contains some of the pre-existing Arabic culture, which it doesn't explain. This is why scholars say that perhaps twenty percent of it cannot be understood today, even by Muslims. We don't have the prior Arabic literature that would shed light on Mohammed's vocabulary and on his rejection of native Arab religious culture.

Parts of the Bible are 1500 years older than the Quran, and all of it is at least 300 years older. That is an advantage when it allows us to trace the steps in the development of the understanding of God, say. For example, it is apparent that the Hebrews had heard the earlier Babylonian myths of creation. There are traces of this mythology used poetically in Job and certain Psalms, where we find mention of Rahab and Leviathan. So they had rejected them by the time Genesis was written. We don't hear anything about Marduk conquering Tiamat and dividing her body into sea and sky. Genesis presents a more rationalized view of creation — more so than the Greeks had at that time.

Monotheism is not necessarily the first thought primitive peoples have. Even the Greeks weren't there yet. The ideas of nature as separate from the spiritual world, of a covenanted society as opposed to kinship, of a universal humanity, of ethical religion as opposed to magic, may seem obvious to us. But we learned them from the Hebrews. And we can watch them learning these things.

Even more important than the fact that the Hebrews' concepts give us a way to think about creation is that they enable Christians to think about Jesus. The concepts we see emerging in the Old Testament are the ones by which Christians understand Jesus, believing that those words found their fullest meaning in him. Words like messiah, sacrifice, miracle, savior, and redeemer may have started out simple, but they became complex. Without them, we would only be able to speak of Jesus as a teacher, which falls far short of what his first followers thought. He would be a puzzle, someone about whom people told strange stories. And he would have been forgotten, like many other such people.

Jesus' followers needed all the concepts mentioned above to express their sense of his unique nature. Concepts they had long been familiar with now came to life. We have the story of Jesus talking to two followers he met incognito after resurrection, where "he interpreted to them in all the scriptures the things concerning himself." They later said, "Did not our hearts burn within us while he talked to us on the road, while he opened to us the scriptures?" (Luke 24). That was the Old Testament they were talking about. It had thrilled them to see the familiar terms of their scriptures materialize in their own lifetimes.

Humanity didn't start out with our religious language, just as it didn't start out with our scientific language. As St. Paul recognized, the Greeks had to learn Judaism before they could understand Christianity. When he visited Athens (Acts 17) he tried to talk to the crowd at Mars Hill in a philosophical language they would recognize. But in his epistles to Jewish and Gentile believers he found it more profitable to develop Old Testament concepts like creation, fall, covenant, judgment, atonement.

A post-Christian culture would insist on using a different vocabulary to account for Jesus. It would insist on the terms of ordinary experience, as we understand it. But such terminology would clearly fail to convey the sense that Christians have made of Jesus and the gospel. It would not begin to explain the way that a small, harried, mixed-race sect conquered the greatest empire Europe had seen.

*　　*　　*

So the long process of the Bible's development was necessary to produce a language that would describe Jesus. Many books, written over a long period of time, were necessary to develop that meaningful complexity. But the next point is about how to get from the Old Testament to the New. Can the two be meaningfully combined as one book? This is obviously an issue between Jews and Christians, who share so many of the same texts and concepts.

H. H. Rowley, a British Old Testament scholar, wrote a book called *The Unity of the Bible* which takes up this problem. Basically his point is that Christians have learned to read the Bible backwards. Rowley fully accepts the differences between Old and New Testaments. But he argues that it is precisely those *differences* that bind them together: "No one could deduce it [the New Testament] from the Old, and there cannot be the slightest suggestion that by the careful study of the Old Testament anyone could have written the New before its history took place. Nevertheless the lines of correspondence are impressive."[4] What he means is that some who have made a serious study of the Old Testament do not recognize Jesus as its fulfillment. They couldn't have predicted Jesus on the basis of Old Testament writings. That's obviously the situation of Judaism; Jews have remained true to older meanings of the common terms and concepts.

But Rowley is saying that after Jesus was actually observed, it became possible to see him as a logical and convincing fulfillment of those concepts, and of the prophecies. When he says that the two parts of scripture are bound together by difference, he means things like Jesus' death being like a sacrifice, but different. The church being like a covenant people, but different. Easter being like Passover, but different. Christian salvation being like ritual atonement, but different.

There are dozens of these analogies or paradoxes. Christians find illumination in reading them backwards. Faith is the ability to put the divine prophecy and the historical reality together, so that one recognizes Jesus as cosmic. It creates a shock of recognition. But perhaps no one could have read them forwards without this experience. The Gospels admit that Jesus' disciples couldn't see these things even when he tried to point them out, but had to be reminded of them afterwards. Even those

4. H. H. Rowley, *The Unity of the Bible* (Cleveland and New York: World Publishing, 1959), 87-92.

who saw Jesus required faith to recognize him as the truth, the church thought.

If the point of the Bible was not to give information, but to create faith, Rowley says this is how it's done. Faith is fostered by the sudden realization that familiar and venerable concepts seem perfectly suited to express such later facts. Such realizations create faith. Faith makes the earlier writings more impressive as well, justifying them as they find convincing fulfillment. It is the same kind of conviction that fulfilled prophecy would create, only in reverse. It gives the confidence that something uncanny is going on here, that the writings carry a Revelation.

So faith is more than biblical literalism. Connecting Jesus with earlier scriptures involved effort — something like a gestalt shift. Christianity does not teach that one is "saved" by belief in stories or principles. It teaches faith in God, and not in the idea of God. Rowley claims that all this comes from learning to read the Bible backwards. To the Christian, Jesus is not kind of like a sacrifice; rather, sacrifices are like Jesus. The older concepts gain their reality, having been shadows before.

*   *   *

This is where Jews and Christians disagree. Jews would hold that Christians are misusing a religious language that had already found its real meaning. They think Jesus' disciples reinterpreted the words in order to cover up a disastrous failure. Rowley's answer to that is to consider the Old Testament in the way Jews do. They will admit two things about it, he says. First, their own books never authorized the Jews to give up the Temple worship that had been commanded. Those sacrifices haven't been going on for two millennia, as we know. So in that sense, Judaism isn't being practiced now. Their scriptures must now be seen as a prologue to the rabbinical scholarship that sustains a scattered people. Second, Rowley points out that Jews admit that the Hebrew scriptures look forward to future developments. The prophecies of a new covenant in people's hearts (Jeremiah), a mission to the Gentiles (Micah), a suffering servant sent to the nations (Isaiah), and outgrowing the racial limits of Judaism (Jonah) still point to the future, on the face of it.

Many Jews would argue that Judaism has moved beyond that most literal sense by now. It has found new referents for these prophecies, new ways of seeing their fulfillment. But we are talking about their scriptures,

136

what Christians call the Old Testament. It would be a help if there had been some literary closure that would explain and approve this. As it is, their scriptures seem to be cut off rather abruptly. Seeing no clear-cut ending to scriptural commands, some Jews would even like to start the sacrificial rites again.

So while the Quran lacks a beginning, the Jewish scriptures seem to lack an ending. Or one can accept the Christian view that the Old Testament prophecies have been completed, but in a way that was not foreseen. Jesus wasn't just a creative individual, teaching a new way to understand Judaism, but a fulfillment beyond all expectations. Christians think there is still more to come, but that they can see the end already. The law is now satisfied; salvation has come.

*   *   *

Rowley suggests that having two parts to scripture can be seen as an advantage. The differences don't seem like contradictions. They are more like paradoxes or creative tensions, in which opposites (like love and judgment, law and grace, works and faith) are both true, and they work together.

Modern secular scholars see things differently. They are absorbed in taking the books apart to study their elements, especially when they sense discrepancies or contradictions. So they contrast Jesus and Paul, Paul and James, Thomas and John, orthodox and Gnostics, to uncover unacknowledged conflicts. Thus their historical reconstructions have more drama. But the church is not surprised, having always known about these tensions. The interesting question is, how did the church overcome them?

The challenge for secular scholarship on the early church is to explain how the early Christian movement held together at all. It outlasted its competition in the religious free-for-all of the Roman Empire, which included as much diversity as our New Age. What was the underlying agreement that gave Christianity its advantage? And how did the tensions become *creative* tensions?

This is where the narrative theology we discussed in the last chapter is relevant. We mentioned scholars like Richard Hays, who try to show how the books fit together. Hays thinks that there is a consistent "moral vision" running through the New Testament books. It can be hard to discern, because the authors don't necessarily employ the same words, ideas, or even principles. What they share is a world of images, metaphors, and examples of life and community.

If one had to choose between ideas and symbols, even philosophers may admit that the images are more potent, flexible, and resilient. In this respect, Hays found three (and only three) themes that run through literally all the books of the New Testament. They are perhaps surprising. Even love and forgiveness are not among them, or are only implied. The three dominant images are the cross, the new creation, and the countercultural community. Of course, the characteristic Christian element of love is involved in them all, but the images give us a way of thinking about love. Hays is inclined to think that we can never exhaust these symbols, that the images are more pregnant than mere concepts. Beyond that, a canon of sources and an emerging narrative is revealed in such agreement.

*   *   *

Academics are now learning how literary canons develop — perhaps learning from the church. As is well known, attacks on the Western literary canon — our lists of "essential" books — have been going on at least since the 1960s. The lists are stigmatized as the work of academic authorities, who force a dead literature on hapless students. Why are no women authors or minorities represented, or those of other spiritualities, the critics ask, when we need to be sensitive to diversity?

Harold Bloom, the prominent English professor, has responded to these concerns in a book called *The Western Canon,* which explains how canons are formed in the first place.[5] To start with, he says, our familiar canon was not just imposed by someone in power. Anyone can make up a list of their favorite books, or of representative authors, but that's not what a canon is. Canons are of a more natural growth — the product of a cultural evolution, as it were.

Our greatest writers know who the earlier great writers were, better than the rest of us do. And their own works consciously or unconsciously respond to them. They test themselves by developing earlier themes or

5. Harold Bloom, *The Western Canon: The Books and School of the Ages* (New York: Riverhead, 1994).

by outdoing their literary heroes. They try to force themselves into the canon, by brilliant effort, forcing it to make room for their own vision. We may think that this process sounds pushy and unpleasant. But Bloom insists that if you want to compete at this level, where only a few authors per century will succeed, that is how it happens.

It adds power to the new books if people have read the earlier giants who are the basis for later efforts. Likewise, it adds to the power of the earlier works, when we see the potential for development of their themes. So the canon is not a sin against originality. It *encourages* originality, not just of an individual but of a whole culture. For the literary canon or tradition is greater than the sum of its parts.

The alternative to writing within a tradition is for authors to "express themselves." But mere self-expression doesn't last. Readers find a couple of favorite authors they enjoy, but will neglect the rest, since authors have no relation to anything bigger than their own works. Each book stands alone, and will soon be forgotten. We have no common culture to discuss. People give up literature, as we have already largely given up poetry.

Bloom thinks the Western literary canon is one of humanity's greatest achievements. He says that it created the category of the human or humanity as we know it. Bloom gives Christian writers — Dante, Milton, and others — credit for contributing, despite his frequently expressed fears of religion. He has shown us that it is better to have many voices in a great chorus, which is what the Bible is. Better than the solo voice we might have thought we would prefer.

PART IV

The University and the Culture Wars

CHAPTER 11

A Brief History of Our Culture Wars

W E ARE not hearing as much about the culture wars as we used to. That doesn't mean there is no struggle going on. In fact, it is entering a new phase, going international. Going ballistic, in fact, so that the wars may not be only metaphorical. We need to put the issue of the university's secularism into the context of these culture wars.

The phrase, of course, was initially a description of what has been happening to American politics in the last fifty years or so. What it means is that whereas politics used to focus on, say, economics and foreign affairs, now it is coming to be more and more about culture. It is still about taxes, budgets, unions, welfare programs, and "creeping socialism," just to name a few topics, but these aren't the hot-button issues anymore. Now the most intractable areas are "cultural issues."

By "culture" we don't mean just high culture or the arts, although the debates in question can have an impact on, say, government funding for the arts. Mostly, we just mean "culture" in the anthropologists' sense — our way of life, the ways of living and thinking that particular societies teach to their children. So that might include, among other things, the educational curriculum, divorce rules, abortion, our attitudes towards drugs or prostitution or pornography, and the way we regard religious expression. This is where people get angriest. It's not so much about how we make a living as about how we live. Or, it's about who we are, or who we want to be. Universities are unable to ignore these conflicts, so they would benefit from a clear-eyed view of the issues involved.

The "wars" part means that it is harder to compromise on these cultural issues than on the economic ones. You can negotiate about money, and accept a little more or a little less. But when you're arguing over individual rights or the social good, it's harder to compromise. Maybe you don't want to destroy your *opponents,* but you want to damage as much as possible their point of view.

The things we can't seem to compromise on are, almost by definition, religious — at least by Paul Tillich's definition, which equates religion with one's "ultimate concern." In the 1992 election, Pat Buchanan got into trouble by calling our politics a "religious war," which seemed like narrow, exclusivist language. But what many didn't realize is that religion is not on just one side of these conflicts. Culture wars reveal the ultimate commitments of all the combatants.

You could probably *define* religion as whatever we can't compromise without losing our personal identity. That's what people dislike about religion. We're uncomfortable with people who can't compromise. Politically, of course, religious persons will submit to being out-voted. That's a different thing. But there's no way they would not use their vote for what they thought is best for everyone.

The political Right won the old politics — the one about economics, taxes, and welfare. Communism and Socialism, at least in their pure forms, are dead. A Democratic president signs off on "welfare reform" and a capital-gains tax cut and announces that the Era of Big Government is over. The British elect a Labour government only after that party repudiates socialism. I'm not saying this is a good thing. That war left a messy battlefield. We haven't solved the problems of the underclass, urban abandonment, or environmental abuse. But these problems do not polarize our body politic the way issues like abortion, gay marriage, or divorce reform do.

In 199 Samuel P. Huntington discussed the international aspect of our subject in *The Clash of Civilizations and the Remaking of World Order.* He was once President's Carter's Director of Security Planning, so he's not a cloistered academic. What Huntington is saying is that our diplomacy is undergoing a similar transformation as our domestic politics, from an economic to a cultural agenda. In the future, he thinks, our international relations may not be primarily about markets and resources, but will be between cultures or civilizations that do not understand or respect each other.

We in the West mistook our victory in the Cold War for the final triumph of modernization. What we now realize, Huntington says, is that we have moved into a new era of civilizational struggles, many of them civil wars. They suggest the re-opening of an era of wars in which sides look for allies among those who share their religious heritage.

We once mistook Afghanistan for a battle in the Cold War. But there have been other such conflicts in Bosnia, Chechnya, Armenia, Indonesia, Sri Lanka, Kashmir, Tajikistan, Sudan, Croatia and Serbia, Israel, the Philippines, Lebanon, and elsewhere. Even European Union politics are snarled over admitting Turkey, whose profession of secularity seems suspect in the West.

Huntington thinks that other areas of the world will *modernize,* but not Westernize. They'll create modern economies and armies, including weapons of mass destruction. And then they'll draw on the resentments built up over centuries, to take Western markets and destroy Western power. China and the Muslim world, especially, may be able to make us accept things on their terms, at their price levels.

In this competition, he says, they will have an advantage because they have preserved their cultures. It is cultures that provide cohesion and justify individual sacrifice. The West has been actively destroying those aspect of its culture in the name of tolerance and multiculturalism, which involved silencing majority groups and effacing their cultural symbols. A few curriculum units on other cultures won't make children multicultural. A culture isn't something to think about, but a way of thinking. Teachers may think they need to encourage a little self-doubt among the majority — part of the old Puritan project of reducing self-esteem. But at what cost?

Meanwhile, Huntington says, we're trusting abstract legal rules to do what culture used to do: hold society together. He thinks it is naïve to think that law or politics can substitute for a thicker culture. He would rather have agreement on what is good, natural, or reasonable than just on the rules of individualized competition.

Whether or not Huntington is right about the world's future, he has raised an important point about our attitude toward cultures. We want other countries to adopt our ways, our list of rights, our freedoms. But we think that Western civilization, or the American way of life, is something to be very suspicious or even ashamed of. In other words, we don't respect foreign cultures, and we don't respect our own. Small wonder if immigrants are becoming reluctant to adopt our ways when we disparage them ourselves.

*   *   *

How did this generalized suspicion of culture become dominant in America? We probably need to take the story back to about 1950. Americans came out of World War II with a large measure of cultural consensus. It would make more sense to call this consensus "liberal" than to call it conservative, given its progressive, optimistic, reformist tone. Eisenhower could have been a candidate for either party in 1952. The Warren Supreme Court, which conservatives later complained of, was largely his creation. Fights went on over economic policy and defense, but the few recognizable conservatives didn't yet have spokesmen who could challenge this liberal cultural consensus. Religious fundamentalists, for example, had no political program. They didn't tend to vote, feeling alienated in many ways from the dominant culture.

Around 1950 things began to change, when a few intellectuals began to complain of "liberal" trends in the universities and "socialism" in the government. These conservatives were the innovators. There was no party that focused on these issues, so they tried to force a debate. Writers like William F. Buckley Jr., Leo Strauss, Richard Weaver, James Burnham, Russell Kirk, and Robert Nisbet began to create an intellectual rationale for their opposition to the trends in American society. In effect, they had to create a conservative tradition. That is not a paradox; historians are familiar with the notion of the manufacture of tradition. And these conservatives weren't creating a tradition from nothing. It's just that people don't think much about the things they take for granted until they're about to lose them. And these writers thought that the threat to America was not just from abroad but also from the internal rot of permissiveness, relativism, and statism.

This New Right grew during the 1950s, and in 1964 it captured the Republican Party long enough to run Barry Goldwater for president. That was just when the Vietnam conflict was heating up, and there was coming to be a New Left too, a more radical element which was trying to capture the Democratic Party. So the culture wars began when there was a real war going on. Maybe that encouraged people to think in those divisive terms.

They didn't take prisoners in the street politics of the 1960s. Students thought the generational difference was unbridgeable and that "you can't trust anyone over 30," even older Democrats. The Right looked at the freakish-looking kids that were the most vocal elements of this New Left and assumed that there wasn't any point in arguing with them. It wasn't a time for discussion, but instead for trading insults and grabbing for political power. We heard a lot of "non-negotiable demands." The raw feelings from that decade are still noticeable among older voters.

The New Left welcomed the Civil Rights movement, along with environmental, economic, and lifestyle issues. But it added up to a general concern. They saw the Vietnam conflict as a sign of American cultural hubris, forcing our ways on all the world when the American way of life had failed here at home. We had racism, sexism, and poverty that we weren't addressing, along with rampant commercialism, obsolete culture standards, and restrictions on drugs and sex that they thought were nobody else's business. In fact, the U.S. had become the enemy of humanity. So the New Left or their allies engaged in violence and civil disobedience in an effort to wreck the war effort at least. Meanwhile, the mainstream "liberals" of both parties were caught in the middle, in shock.

If we had to put these two positions on bumper-stickers, we would probably say that the Right emphasized responsibility while the Left emphasized freedom. Or that the Right was concerned with societal cohesion while the Left was concerned with individual rights. But that was only on the cultural issues. On the economic issues these were exactly reversed. There, the Right wanted individual freedoms (as against government regulation) while the Left wanted social responsibility (in the form of economic regulation). You might wonder why the two sides couldn't be consistent — wanting either social responsibility or individual freedom across the board. And actually there are very small groups that are more consistent — the "communitarians" for responsibility, and the "libertarians" for freedom. But we don't hear much about their ideas, because they have never become politically important.

Perhaps our inconsistency here makes a certain kind of sense. It may be our way of recognizing that you can't absolutize either freedom or responsibility. You can't absolutize either society or the individual. They need to be in tension with each other. There's got to be some balancing of freedom and responsibility.

*　　*　　*

In the early 1970s the Vietnam War ended and the country settled down a bit. The New Left passed its thirtieth birthday and was co-opted into university faculties, the media, government bureaucracies, and denominational headquarters. But the New Right felt repudiated. It wasn't represented anywhere in the Establishment. It hadn't even captured the Republican Party, where Nixon kept it at arm's length. But it was finding a base in religion. Apparently that happened when religious schools sprang up to protest court-ordered desegregation and were hassled by federal and state governments and the press. The New Right began to counterattack, criticizing the public school curriculum, sex education, drugs in the schools, and low educational performance. Then, in the late 1970s, when televangelism was born, the IRS, SEC, and FCC began to lean on them as well, checking their licenses and fundraising. Suddenly these religious leaders discovered that they could call on a lot of support from the public, and this became the basis for the Moral Majority in the 1980 election. The Right rejected President Carter, who was transparently more religious than Reagan, because he didn't speak their cultural language.

In the view of the media at least, the New Right became largely a religious movement after that. This had not been the case earlier. At the same time we began to notice that religion seemed to be on the rise as a potent force in Iran, India, Poland, and a lot of other places in the world, to the surprise of social scientists everywhere.

Meanwhile, the Democratic Party was edging away from religion. In the early 1970s, the more radical element that was taking over decided that the old alliance with blue-collar workers, Catholics, and white southerners was less promising than an appeal to a growing number of cultural liberals. This group was less interested in religion, and as the Right become more so, there was a reaction toward a distinctly secular perspective on certain issues.

By 1990 the differences were so wide that academics started paying attention. A sociologist at the University of Virginia, James Davison Hunter, issued the most comprehensive report in a book entitled *Culture Wars: The Struggle to Define America*.[1] He identified five broad is-

1. James Davison Hunter, *Culture Wars: The Struggle to Define America* (New York: Basic Books, 1991).

sues being contested: the family, education, the media, law, and political debate.

Family is enormously important in modern life in an emotional sense, as other social groups like unions, neighborhoods, churches, and lodges fade to memories. There is no more potent image in our advertisements than that of family. This has been the Right's issue, because family stands for continuity with the past and sacrifice for the future. For the Left, family has become entangled in the "rights revolution." A concentration on rights leads to defining our relationships legally rather than handling them informally in the context of family. We get away from traditional notions of good, natural, or reasonable when we legalize them. Rights are created precisely in order to be used *against* old habits. At present we are legalizing the whole range of our personal relations, out of a distrust of customary relationships.

Just now the issue is same-sex marriage. On what basis can we deny people that right? The fear is that the same logic will raise the question of whether there is a right to polygamy, if three or four people want a group marriage, say. Then it will be incest among consenting adults. At each step in this progression the question will be, on what rationale would society deny that right, if it doesn't affect other people's right to do what they want?

Such questions didn't come up when we were more in agreement on what was natural and reasonable in life — when culture ruled. In 1890 the Supreme Court (in *Davis v. Beeson*) ruled against the Mormons on polygamy, saying it was uncivilized. But the idea of "civilization" no longer has any legal force. Are there cultural constraints or moral imperatives or natural guidelines that we should take as seriously as constitutional amendments? Are there natural, defining characteristics of society that predate the state and are above its reach? And who is to say? Wouldn't they actually be religious, and thus controversial and polarizing in the political realm?

We still have a great measure of agreement on what is reasonable. But all it takes is for one person to raise a question about something we all thought was settled. That legal challenge then becomes part of a civil suit, and some judge will have to search constitutional law to see if its wording could be used to break up our customary habits.

There is always a three-way power struggle going on during these episodes, three sources of authority. *Culture* is still a force. It's a form of democracy, involving past generations as well as the present. And it still gets a certain amount of respect. *Democracy* itself is a force, meaning this week's majority. We think that's our basic method, but Americans have always been suspicious of majorities and have built up safeguards against them. So we have *judges,* who may feel they must invoke the Constitution over both today's democracy and yesterday's custom.

All three of these authorities are being criticized these days. Cultural tradition is suspect, since calling something "traditional" suggests that it has lost its original rationale or legitimacy. If marriage is only traditional — and now only relevant to the tax laws — maybe we should do away with it altogether. Democracy is discredited by the behavior of our elected officials, or at least by the media's relentless criticism of them. And there's a big debate over whether judges are practicing judicial tyranny — trying to legislate for us. Critics of the judiciary point to *Roe v. Wade,* in which the Court majority decreed that voters and state legislatures could not legislate on abortion.

Religion is not a separate force in this tug-of-war. Religion is part of culture. Its values and presuppositions run the whole gamut of the democratic electorate — to the left as well as the right, even if the New Left, as we saw earlier, eschewed much of *traditional* religion. And religion has often depended on judges and constitutional guarantees. In fact, minority religions have often pioneered in the establishment of our minority rights, often against dominant religions. So religion complicates every facet of the culture wars — which is not necessarily a bad thing, since complicated questions are involved.

Hunter also pointed to the issues surrounding education. These are familiar enough: fights over the curriculum and the canon of core literature, values clarification as a substitute for moral insistence, sex education, cultural relativism, and multiculturalism. Basically, the question is not whose culture is taught but whether we can have an education that is culture-free, and which concentrates entirely on skills. We may think this is necessary, since we are divided on cultural issues. So we are undertaking an experiment in education without reference to basic beliefs.

It might seem that pragmatism and tolerance constitute the foundations of this project. But they only beg the question. After all, you can't insist on tolerance; that would be intolerant. Tolerance might be your personal value, but should you force it on others? Furthermore, nobody seriously believes we're going to tolerate *everything.* We could probe and find our basic beliefs, but will we then have the nerve to insist on them? If not, how can we justify forcing kids to come to schools?

The Left has foundational beliefs, and when we explore them they will look more like religious commitments than like pragmatism. The supreme pragmatist, John Dewey, recognized this when he titled his book *A Common Faith* (1934), and it was the Supreme Court that first called "secular humanism" a religion (*Torcaso v. Watkins*, 1961). So the issue really is whose tolerance will be imposed on whom.

The media are just as important as education in our cultural skirmishes. Education provides information and skills, but the media tells our stories, which govern the way we think about our lives and about ourselves. The Left doesn't see a problem with a free press. But the Right has noticed that the media are deciding the stories we are *not* supposed to tell. If you don't own a newspaper chain or a movie studio or a publishing house or television network, you may not ever see your views treated fairly, or treated at all. In other words, it is the corporate media that are the major censors nowadays.

Actually, the media are as conflicted as the rest of us are. Television stations editorialize about gun control while filling our entertainment with violence. Entertainment seems to promote a sexual revolution even while showing the most prurient interest in sexual misconduct. The news laments the decline of our political campaigning while carrying the political commercials that degrade it. And it complains of the cost of electioneering while raising advertising rates for candidates.

Law is a major battleground as well. Nearly $15 million was spent to defeat Robert Bork's nomination to the Supreme Court. We have already discussed how rights become implicated in an anti-cultural project. As these campaigns proceed in the teeth of cultural opposition, we all become more aware of the naked power involved. And as our laws are no longer internalized in custom, the courts become busier.

Finally, Hunter mentions politics, by which he means debates over what kinds of arguments we are allowed to use. Are we allowed to voice our private religious views in public argument, for instance? After all, these are not universally shared. The way we usually speak of this is to complain that people are imposing their beliefs on others. That's a confused notion. In the first place, you can't impose beliefs, but only behaviors. Second, democratic politics is always motivated by beliefs. What else is there to guide us? Third, politics always imposes the will of some on others. That's the nature of democracy. And fourth, the idea that any voter can impose anything on everybody else is not realistic. We each have one vote, and we use it for what we think will be best for everyone. Everyone else has one vote, and uses it for what they think will be best for everyone. Democracy is the process of shaking these votes down and discovering where the weight lies. We don't require people to explain their votes. So the idea that one should not "impose one's beliefs" seems to be an effort to rule certain beliefs out of order, so that other beliefs may rule. As I said in chapter eight, so long as a law doesn't require a religion or prohibit one, there shouldn't be a problem.

*   *   *

A cultural politics is made worse by several characteristics of our society. Sociologists like Peter Berger relate the culture wars to the emergence of what they call the "New Class."[2] Since World War II, the U.S. economy has shifted from industrial production to the service sector, and more recently to information-based services. The education, communications, and therapy sectors have grown enormously and produced a new middle class that is not at all like the old one. The old middle class meant businessmen, and it valued enterprise, economic freedom, personal authority. The new knowledge professionals are more attuned to the bureaucratic virtues, and identify with government and the educational establishment. The "New Class" may be in the process of displacing the old establishment.

Another thing that encourages conflict is that our society is so media-driven. Media profits depend on conflict, so their reports are undoubtedly more polarized than the public itself. Of course, the media use polling to justify their polarized picture, but they may structure that polling to sharpen the issues. Who would guess that there are a dozen different positions on abortion out there?

Victories in the culture wars are often registered in the laws that are passed or the elections won. But they are also seen when they capture the words that we use. The phrase "family values" has been successfully captured by conservatives, despite liberal claims of its hollowness. The

2. Peter L. Berger, *A Far Glory: The Quest for Faith in an Age of Credulity* (New York: Doubleday, 1993), 51-62.

phrase "political correctness" has been worth whole regiments. By contrast, liberals have neutralized the appeal to morality by raising the question of "whose morality?" Talk of the "Religious Right" is frightening to many. The talk of "rights" — a liberal concept — so dominates our social philosophy that conservatives are forced to re-conceptualize even traditions in those terms. Our visceral opposition to pornography, for example, must be put in terms of women's rights — a sometimes awkward reformulation of a long-held cultural value.

The Right expected great things when President Reagan seemed receptive to its cultural agenda. Conservatives poured into Washington, despite all the disparaging things they'd said about that town. They set up think tanks and policy institutes and opinion journals to rival those of the Left. They pioneered political action committees to outflank the parties. They invented direct mail solicitation to outflank the news media in getting out their information. And they invented political talk radio to counter the liberal networks. So the Right now has the same sort of institutional base that the Left seized from a faltering liberal establishment. Endowing and staffing such institutions give the warring positions a permanence that the force of ideas alone might not provide.

The Left, meanwhile, has institutionalized itself in the universities to a much greater degree than the Right, at least in those departments that would have anything to say on cultural issues. But the Left may have overplayed its hand. They have spread a certain anti-intellectualism in promoting the assumption that ideas mainly reflect one's race, class, gender, or ethnicity, and that Western-style argumentation is therefore futile. Why even *have* universities if that is true?

Conservatives have enjoyed postmodernism's mishaps, like the outing of Paul de Man as a fascist collaborator and the "post-modernist physics" hoax perpetrated on the journal *Social Text*.[3] For conservatives view all this as a split within an incoherent liberalism, and they encourage the public to associate all this with the most outrageous claims for diversity.

Meanwhile, the federal funding which universities had hoped would grow may be dwindling, as a sign that universities are losing their social weight and are not worth fighting over. The mainstream media show

3. See *Quick Studies: The Best of Lingua Franca,* ed. Alesander Star (New York: Farrar, Straus and Giroux, 2002), xvii-xix, 3-9.

signs of losing their importance as well. Newspaper readership is falling faster than church attendance, and alternative media are hardly a substitute in any kind of bonding role.

*   *   *

How are the culture wars affecting the churches? There was a religious element in our culture wars from the very beginning. An increased awareness of other religions was part of the 1960s — including Asian traditions, Native American religions, and drug-induced mystical states. The lapse of immigration quotas in 1965 opened up our society religiously as well as culturally. Government has gone to great lengths to avoid the appearance of religious favoritism — and in the process turned to a conscientious secularism. Churches, especially traditionalist ones, have sensed a greater and greater cultural threat.

When the federal bureaucracy began to harass the televangelists, they found a surprising backlash. This in turn generated a reaction from churches on the Left. Mainstream denominations had long accepted an officially liberal agenda — of disarmament, civil rights, environmental concerns, and attention to world hunger. They rarely gave leadership to that liberal agenda, but it seemed close enough to their views that they thought it should be supported. In reaction against religions to the right of them, they got into the cultural sphere on the other side on such issues as school prayer. So the Religious Left feels threatened now.

Every denomination found itself split over the new politics. All major denominations saw the organization of conservative action groups during the 1960s and 1970s. There were fights over denominational offices, agencies, and budgets. As a result, religious identities may now center on parachurch ministries or particular religious periodicals, authors, or charities, rather than on denominations. Hunter also notices that alliances have formed between the conservative wings of different denominations and even of different faiths, which would have been unthinkable earlier. Similarly, liberal Catholics, Jews, and Protestants are cooperating as co-belligerents.

There is also an important division between clergy and laity. New Class theory suggests that clergy in denominational bureaucracies and seminaries will represent the knowledge class, with its current affinity for a liberal stance. But donations come more from the old middle class, and have increasingly been withheld. The mainline churches are more likely than conservative churches to be split along these clerical/lay lines.

*   *   *

In all of this division, we may need reminding that religion is more than culture. Theological liberals are officially suspicious of traditional culture, having been taught that cultural shells must to be cracked open to find the truths within. Although they recognize that truth is always expressed in cultural terms, they know that one must treat religion metaphorically. The challenge is finding an alternative to cultural traditions that will motivate the laity, short of politics itself.

Religious conservatives, on the other hand, may be defending a culture instead of a faith. Often being on the outside of dominant academic views, they need to become aware of how liberal culture was proposed as a sort of substitute for religious faith. But this happened long ago, and the culture they inherited, formed by Protestant liberalism at the time of the beginning of universities, has come to seem religious in retrospect.

Those who confuse Americanism and Protestant Christianity would be surprised at how what we now view as the safe standards of our grandparents were originally looked at askance. At the birth of the liberal educational curriculum, secularists hoped that art and literature of a certain quality would awaken the awe and reverence that had been the task of religion in previous times. So the Right needs to discover the independence of religious faith from cultural forms. Perhaps they worry so much about the public schools because they mistake them for churches. They despair of our laws because they take them to be moral doctrines. They worry about art because they think it is a kind of worship. They worry about the news because they feel like they are being preached to.

They are right to be concerned. But they should realize that their religious identity is not likely to feel comfortable in any human culture. And yet, as I argued in chapter four, the secularization of some aspects of life allows the greater spiritualization of other aspects, as we revive the vital sense that religion transcends any culture.

CHAPTER 12

The Child as Secular Icon

I N THE present state of American culture we often react more strongly to images and symbols than to ideas or arguments. Whether this has always been true, it would seem to reflect the rise of television and decline of print. And one of the objectives of culture warriors is to become guardians of the major symbols of our common life.

If one pays attention to the media, it appears that our main image of the good is the child. Our most uncontroversial way to introduce moral judgments is to refer to children's needs. Television ads offer ample evidence that our children's good is an uncontested value. We may belie this in practice; it appears, for example, that the average time adults spend with children is dropping. Children spend an increasing amount of their lives thrown together with age-mates or electronic companionship. Perhaps as compensation, adults burnish an image of childhood that amounts to something like a cultural idol. But phrasing it that way brings us back around to religion. Is the good of children primarily a secular value or a religious one? Who gets the credit, in our cultural rivalry, as patrons of the child? Has religion ever really promoted children's welfare, or has it mostly been a source of problems? Popular historians suggest that religion was the snake in some children's paradise. So if children are a natural symbol of all that is good, innocent, promising, and creative, is there even a need for religious symbols of the good anymore?

There was a time in the 1960s when it briefly appeared that universities would take up the history of children and the image of childhood in a serious way, uncovering the cultural aspects of the subject as a window into understanding ourselves.[1] That moment passed when the history of women and of feminism stepped into the foreground instead. This was understandable, but the study of women and of children, oddly, did not seem to be able to flourish together. Indeed they found themselves to be rivals. The result was that only a rather amateur historiography of childhood survived in universities.

*   *   *

First, we need to recognize that our culture's image of The Child is a different thing from the actual children that get in our way in the mall and cause parents and journalists and school administrators such vexation. The image we cherish is of children at their best, which remains an ideal as much as a reality. For what we actually mean by The Child probably doesn't refer to the young persons in our midst so much as to *ourselves* as children. The child that fills our imagination is likely made up of memories of ourselves at that age. This allows a disconnect between our expressions of concern and such measures as the time we devote to them.

This was apparent in the first person in Western history who was identified with the child's interests and needs, Jean-Jacques Rousseau. Until Rousseau's time, in the 1760s, his fellow writers and philosophers had viewed children as potential humans, who required shaping for fear that nature might never be socialized. All the resources of civilization were brought to bear in this effort. Rousseau was exceptional in his time for taking the opposite view. He presented children as the pristine image of human nature, who must be protected from the heavy hand of civilization if they were to flourish. Civilization was the source of evil, not nature. This turned Western values on their head. From fearing the power of natural instincts, Europeans began to fear the crushing power of society. This became a major cultural watershed in the history of the West.

Before Rousseau's time there had been some in Western societies who had expressed a realistic sympathy for children. As early as Roman

1. The reading list for the first course I taught on the subject included Philippe Ariès, *Centuries of Childhood* ((New York: Vintage, 1962), Edmund Morgan, *The Puritan Family* (New York: Harper, 1966), Urie Bronfenbrenner, *Two Worlds of Childhood* (New York: Sage, 1970), Erik Erikson, *Childhood and Society* (New York: Norton, 1963), Peter Coveney, *The Image of Childhood* (Harmondsworth: Penguin, 1967), and E. A. Wrigley, *Population and History* (New York: McGraw-Hill, 1969).

times, there were notable efforts to make parents aware of their responsibilities, in writings by Plutarch and Quintilian and legislation by Augustus.[2] The problem was that this concern was directed only toward upper-class children. It was compatible with child slavery and a certain amount of infanticide, for instance. In reality, the concern was for the family that these children would one day serve or lead. Much later, John Locke had been notable for taking a quite realistic view of the child's needs in a remarkable book, *Some Thoughts Concerning Education* (1693). He did not think the child came into the world "from afar . . . trailing clouds of glory," as Wordsworth was later to say. Rather, Locke was famous for his image of the child as a "blank tablet" upon which experience would inscribe its lessons. The book must have struck a chord in eighteenth-century Europe, enjoying at least twenty-six editions in English, sixteen in French, six in Italian, and others in Dutch, German, Swedish, and Spanish. Books achieve this level of popularity not because they are original and controversial, but because the public is predisposed to agree with them. We will see how that had come about a little later.

Rousseau was different. He really was controversial, as he meant to be. His book *Emile* (1762) was argued over for generations. The great philosopher Immanuel Kant could not put it down, and missed his daily walk for three days — a major event in his methodical life. What the public read in it violated their assumptions in every way. The fictional boy Emile was tutored by a man who gave him absolute freedom, out of a conviction that motivation is key to education. The child learned at his own pace. He never went to school and saw no point in learning to read until far past the age when Europeans started drilling their children. When he did decide he wanted to read the books his tutor was mentioning, he learned in a flash. He took up various subjects as they presented themselves to his attention, and by his middle teens he had progressed through math and science and was embarked on his moral education in literature and history. He had never been forced along and therefore harbored no resentment of his tutor or of adults in general. By age twenty-two he was ready to see the world and was taken on a tour, in which he met the leaders of the countries that he would be dealing with in his likely role as a diplomat or politician. For he had left his age-mates far

2. See C. John Sommerville, *The Rise and Fall of Childhood* (New York: Random House, 1990).

behind, as they struggled through their problems with submission and resentment — things that had never been generated in Emile.

The book shows a truly original ability to enter into a child's mind. But many thought it was unrealistic to think that the waywardness of human nature would not cause the usual problems. Had they known Rousseau personally, they would have had other reasons to wonder about the work. For he was obviously one who was using the child's image to wrestle with his personal problems. Rousseau had not had satisfactory relations with women and never married. He fathered at least five children, all of whom he abandoned to the local orphanage, and it is perhaps fortunate that he did not leave the world his example of parenting. In his frank autobiography he admitted his rages over his pupil's insubordination and sloth. Paranoia may have driven him to suicide, if that is indeed the explanation of his early death.

Rousseau felt guilty and ashamed of his desire to dominate others, to counter the paranoid threats he imagined. This shame prompted him to create an educational method which apparently did not rely on authority. He found the needed authority in nature itself, and rejoiced in showing how nature took its revenge on Emile's thoughtlessness.

It is hard to believe that Rousseau cared anything for the actual effect of his work, so long as it established his literary reputation. He never addressed the practical problems involved in his educational program and secretly ridiculed those who tried to rear their children by his precepts. If taken seriously, the book would make the job of the sensitive parent all but impossible, with its frequent warnings that some slip "may destroy six months' work and do irreparable damage for life." This was just one more way for his sadism to create guilt in others.

*   *   *

Something of this same explanation might be given for the many novelists and children's authors who followed in Rousseau's wake. For in the early nineteenth century the innocent child became a major theme of adult novels and the earliest published children's stories. The children in the novels of Charles Dickens, George Eliot, Charlotte Brontë, and many others are beyond unbelievable. They are merely the victims and reflections of the misconduct and meanness of adults. When they die, as so many of them do, it is a judgment on those adults. And so long as they live, the world we see through their eyes is a world of crushing evil, which the authors mean us to reject. It is the world of the industrial revolution, of the rising bourgeoisie and evangelical religion, which offended authors who aspired to genteel cultivation. But the pathos of the child characters may have had more to do with the authors' self-obsession than with social reality.

The sentimentality with which these child characters are treated makes them seem perfectly unreal. They were not drawn from life, but from the authors' imaginations, and perhaps from their self-pity. Fictional children were dying in record numbers at the same time actual child mortality was declining noticeably. These authors seemed to be using the child as a weapon in their struggle against unattractive social change.

The most obvious targets of this hostility were the fictional schools the children attended. And of course schools in the early nineteenth century were invariably religious, as Western governments had not gotten around to tax-supported education.

From the generation of those authors, there has been a growing sense that religion is tantamount to child abuse. If one accepts a "Romanticist" philosophy of naturalistic primitivism, religion falls into the category of what is unnatural and irrational. There are classic scenes in those novels in which harshly religious schoolmasters labor to estrange children from the natural sources of goodness. The children's natural goodness alone can triumph over such evil. Many of them have no family to speak of, or other supports outside of themselves, but they find the inner resources to stand up to what religious cultures represent. This literary theme was a victory for a secular naturalism in the early stages of a culture war.

We should remember one other thing about these Victorians. While the Victorian period sentimentalized the child as never before, we might remember that "Victorian" has become a catchword for psychological repression. It is no accident that depth psychology was born in such a culture. For the hardest work that children have ever had to do was to symbolize innocence. Freud's patients, and their parents, were presumably immersed in the culture represented by this literature.

Freud represents a later age, a time when science demythologized the secular religion of the innocent child. Whatever is now thought of his particular theories, he was more realistic than the cult of childhood innocence that had gone before. He had this, at least, in common with earlier religious views: neither of them thought the child benefitted from being idolized.

*　　*　　*

In fact, the ancient myths that Freud thought reflected his views, the Oedipus Complex and others, take us back to an ancient world. It was in this world that the Christian church first debated the nature of childhood. We find something like the same quarrel over spiritual nature and spiritual nurture in the church of Jerome and Augustine, about AD 400. St. Jerome wrote some famous letters on the raising of girls within the church. They are very tender letters and concerned to make education pleasant. But their constant theme was protecting the child's supposed innocence. All the girls' instincts were to be repressed, so that they would be fit to become nuns when they were grown. For that was his ideal of adulthood. St. Augustine, by contrast, wrote an autobiography to show how unrealistic that was. In the *Confessions* he remembered how eager he was to be rebellious at an early age. The famous episode of his stealing the pears represents only the worst thing he could think of, young as he was. It only showed how determined he was to be true to his wayward nature, by repeating the original sin, deciding for himself among the fruits of the knowledge of good and evil rather than living within God's will.

Augustine was not saying that children were worse than adults. Rather, he was making Freud's point that adult traits can be traced all the way back to one's earliest years. No earlier author had taken children seriously as moral beings. In the end, the church tried to compromise these views, accepting Augustine's philosophical formulation of human fallenness (in the transmission of original sin) and also Jerome's view of the practical innocence of the child (by baptism) up to an age of personal accountability. Christians may have muddled both of these views, emphasizing one and then another, but they were beginning the Western debate over the issues of childhood.

*　　*　　*

The social history of children is a depressing story. Adults have always wanted to shift the job of child-rearing to others, for it has never seemed

161

an exalted job. The wealthiest have the worst record of neglect, having the most resources to carry out this wish. Religious thinkers, by contrast, have historically shown the most concern.

As a British historian, it was clear to me that the first group that was noted for an interest in children, both boys and girls, were . . . the Puritans. Of all people! Puritans have such a poor reputation in so many history books. But far too many historians have not done their homework. If they made a close study of the Puritan attention to children, they would be in for a surprise.[3]

There is a ready explanation for this Puritan interest in children. It is not that they needed victims for their repressed psyches, or that they were expressing bourgeois inhibitions, or that they had an anti-humanist theology. If it had been any of these, their interest would have taken different forms. Rather, their attention to childhood stemmed from the fact that Puritanism was a social movement. In its original conception, Puritanism was a movement to change society, but it had little or no standing within the institutions of that society. Americans think of Puritans as the Establishment in their tiny outpost in Massachusetts Bay. But the reason they had settled in that wilderness was that they had fled from being harassed in England. Over there, they were an ostracized minority. As such, if they were ever to succeed as a movement, in the absence of institutionalized power, they would need to capture the rising generation.

The Puritans hoped to change their society, and the name derives from their plans to purify the Church of England so that it would be more coherent and spiritual. Churches were involved with all areas of life at that time, so this would mean a general social and political reform. There was much in English life that needed reform, and the Puritans were remarkably modern in many of their attitudes. Some of them envisioned certain individual freedoms, science in the curriculum, reform of an archaic legal system and family law, less brutal schools, democratic reforms in the church, honesty in government, and equality before the law. And it is never long before such reform movements realize that "children are the future."

Being religious, they thought that if Christian values began to per-

<hr/>

3. C. John Sommerville, *The Discovery of Childhood in Puritan England* (Athens: University of Georgia Press, 1992).

vade all of society, everyone would see the beauty of the change. You see this in the new names they gave to their children. Before Queen Elizabeth's reign, children were given the names of their parents and relatives. The names were just labels, meaning nothing in particular. There were only a few dozen names for boys and a like number for girls until the Puritans began to search the Bible for names that could be something to live up to. Hebrew names had meanings, as they knew, and sometimes the Puritans simply left these in their English forms, like Grace, Prudence, Mercy, Joy, Praise-God, and Thankful. The new names signified the new age that reform would bring.

Once they had given their children these names, they wrote books to tell parents how to raise these new people. All of the books of child-rearing advice until Locke's time were by this minority group of Puritans. They were usually by clergymen and were not as insightful as Locke's later work, but then he had their examples to build on. (He may have grown up in a Puritan household.) All of them urged mothers to nurse their own children, at a time when many children were left with nurses from the lowest classes. They complained of parents' neglect, which often took the form of indulging the children. The trouble with spoiling children, they said, is that they are no fun to have around later, and physical violence is likely to be the result. They urged parents to be more consistent and thoughtful in discipline, which might make it less harsh in the long run. Spanking would sometimes be necessary, but it should not be in anger, just to vent the parent's rage. They urged that punishment aim at a change in behavior, and that if "admonishing" would make the change, parents should stop at that. Remember, they said, you passed on a wayward nature to your children, so you have yourself to blame as well. This should make you sympathetic.[4]

This doctrine of the transmission of a fallen nature horrifies historians who have no desire to be fair to the Puritans. They may hear that the child-rearing manuals mention spanking, and assume that Puritans invented the practice. You don't read about spanking in non-Puritan manuals of the time — because there aren't any. The Puritans had observed that people generally were perfectly thoughtless and brutal in their treatment of children, and needed to be awakened to sympathy. In this respect, they were the first modern parents.

4. Sommerville, *The Discovery of Childhood*, 30.

Whether the Puritans actually followed their books is not clear, any more than whether we follow the best advice we get today. But the number and sale of these manuals shows that many saw the problem and wanted to be thoughtful parents. They probably shared the same instincts as their neighbors, but if book-buying habits are any indication, they differed in the amount of attention they gave to their task.

As the children grew up, Puritan authors wrote books to interest them. There had been printed ballads before that were enjoyed by all ages. We may mistake them for children's books. But in fact, the first books published specifically for children were by Puritans, and there is quite a variety of them. All of them had a religious intent, so many scholars refuse to acknowledge them as true children's literature. But the very fact that they were produced for, and perhaps read to, children would have been a message by itself. It showed the children that they were worthy of that benign attention from grown-ups. The books included allegories, verses, Bible story books, stories about real children, and even plays, at a time when Puritans objected to the level to which the theater had fallen after Shakespeare's time. They also pioneered in writing "programmed" and illustrated educational materials, something that was forgotten in subsequent centuries. It can also be shown that Puritan "covenant theology" itself changed in response to their concern for children.

Why don't the Puritans get more credit? Partly it is because this story had a sad ending. Puritanism failed in its attempt to achieve power and use it for good. The restored monarchy made them suffer for their continued non-conformity. And when they lost hope for success, their educational program made less sense. They were understandably embittered, and they may have taken it out on their children. For example, during the seventeenth century, when there was still hope for the movement, you do not read about "breaking the child's will." That language became current in the eighteenth century, and even appears in Locke. This was a time when social conservatives were back in power, the future was not a focus, and we don't hear much about children. Historian Linda Pollock has made the only real effort to make a systematic study of the evidence for physical punishment through this long period, through a study of English diaries. She found a considerable continuity in the actual treatment of children. She couldn't show either a rise in affections or a decrease in spanking. But she noticed a notably harsher discipline in

England in the early nineteenth century, when Puritans were long gone and Rousseau's disciples held sway.[5]

So things may not be as they appear. Those who romanticized the child in literature may have had little to do with actual children, even their own. And those whose theology may repel us may have been more engaged with and thoughtful toward them.

*   *   *

The position of children in the "over-developed" secular societies of today should certainly give us pause. Kids face absolutely unprecedented difficulties which we largely ignore. There has never been a time when the social institutions that are concerned with children were so uncoordinated with each other. Families are often pitted against schools. Schools should be pitted against the entertainment industry. Churches are at odds with entertainment, and sometimes with schools. Peer groups are at odds with schools and families. The world of work may compete with all of these. The Internet exerts a pull in destructive directions.

Meanwhile, many children have freedoms well beyond what they can handle without guidance and support. Unfortunately, this guidance often comes up against the power of the state, which wants families to be accountable to it. The ever-growing state may have the best of intentions, but it cannot actually administer its own mandates. The state cannot hug a child or be a role model. While it can make spanking a misdemeanor, it will be unable to offer the substitutions that might be necessary.

Another unprecedented change is that some states seem determined to neutralize the transmission of culture, even if this means alienating the majority from its cultural heritage and history. Political elites may decide there are elements in the dominant culture that we should outgrow. The definition of "culturally disadvantaged families" can grow to suit their agendas. Since diversity cannot be taught, we settle instead for disparaging our heritage, in light of its offenses. Schools are less sure than ever of what they should be teaching and now settle for transmitting job skills. It is another evidence of the principle that the state is often better at destroying than at creating.

---

5. Linda A. Pollock, *Forgotten Children: Parent-Child Relations from 1500 to 1900* (Cambridge: Cambridge University Press, 1983), 184f., 197, 269.

*   *   *

It seems incontestable that treatment of children is the best measure of the worth of a civilization. Children are the most truly helpless persons in view, and we should gauge our society by how we treat those who are most completely in our power. The status and pay of those who work with children has always been deplorably low. Women are made to feel that a "real" job is a step up from raising children. And as between religious and secular mindsets on the subject, there are many things to consider.

Religions may differ in their concern for children, and some of them may have changed over time. Some seem to tolerate child labor, child slavery, child soldiers, and even using children as human bombs. Secularism has not yet developed a position it can call its own. This is a time when many millions more are aborted than seems absolutely necessary — if we can even agree on what "necessary" means in this context. And those who survive the abortion decision are not assured that they are really "wanted"; indeed, over ninety percent of the abusive parents in one study claimed that they had "planned" the child. We "want" children for all sorts of reasons, good and bad. And planned children can be a bigger disappointment to their parents, for any number of reasons.

It is a time when many are born HIV-positive or in drug withdrawal, a time when religious leaders have become involved in a culture of pedophilia, and a time when liberal ideology sometimes strains to condemn such abhorrent sexual behavior. It is a time when rising figures on child abuse are assumed to represent a rise in sensitivity on the issue — meaning we find a way to pat ourselves on the back in the face of the grimmest of statistics.

For that matter, have we ever thought how they get children to act in those television ads? We only see the children smiling and happy. How much unhappiness and actual rage were left on the cutting-room floor? And how were the child labor laws adjusted for this commercial and cultural purpose? How much has really changed in that respect in the hundred years since child circus-performers were exempted from the flexible child-labor laws of that time?

It has often taken religion to teach us what now seem very commonplace attitudes toward child welfare.[6] But we will face unprecedented

---

6. This is a theme of my *Rise and Fall of Childhood.*

challenges as we gain more control over their genetic composition in the coming age of "designer children." Karen Peterson-Iyer has surveyed the current literature on this subject in *Designer Children: Reconciling Genetic Technology, Feminism, and Christian Faith.* Her list of concerns is sobering. They include the facts that gene-line engineering affects the individuals' descendants too, that we cannot assume we know all the side effects, that it will raise parental hopes unrealistically, increase our intolerance of difference, increase class divisions and the advantages of wealth, divert research resources from more widespread needs, and may be mandated politically. Most troubling is that we will begin to "value" children as objects or property rather than respect them as persons. Children are in danger of being *accepted* conditionally and on the basis of our desires rather than *loved* for themselves, in all their individuality.[7] We have seen these abuses before, but they will become almost unavoidable the more we take a hand in our genetic therapy, and then in genetic "enhancement."

Christians have a ground for their concepts of love, responsibility, thankfulness, dignity, and their acceptance of nature as a given. They recognize that they are not the only creators. Their moral perspective is not limited to the secular goals of freedom and chosen relationships.[8] They should be able to maintain the concept of persons as ends with less hesitation than those without an ultimate reference. When the university must address such questions, it would be tragic if it stifled such voices out of a concern that religion is too controversial, too polarizing, or too outdated. For this is one area in which society needs all the help it can get.

7. Karen Peterson-Iyer, *Designer Children: Reconciling Genetic Technology, Feminism, and Christian Faith* (Cleveland: Pilgrim, 2004), 23-35, 43.

8. Peterson-Iyer, *Designer Children,* 114.

CHAPTER 13

News as Culture Substitute

J UST AS a secular culture has its symbols of the good, like the child, so
it has its standard sources of knowledge. In this chapter we will look at
the degree to which the news media qualify as a legitimate source, and
what their effects have been. For there seem to be dangers in allowing
news to substitute for other elements of a discredited culture, or for culture generally.

When the secular university was first being developed, intellectuals
disdained newspapers as fodder for the lower classes, or at least for the
less reflective part of respectable society. Newspapers were dismissed as
dealing in sensationalism and the merely practical side of life. Journalism has changed since then. It has at least become more diverse. Not all
media are aimed at a mass audience, and some do address cultural issues in a serious way. There are reviews appearing on a monthly or quar-
terly basis, and this has led to the idea that one can keep abreast of intellectual changes by reading little that is not periodical. So even
academics now take being "informed" seriously, in something like the
sense that spiritual disciplines were once followed. Given the pace of
change, this becomes more demanding all the time.

It may have escaped us how this marks a change in the position of
universities within America's intellectual and cultural life. The public
looks to the media and now to the Internet for what it once found in
books and in the academy. Faculty also devote more attention to the media, to find what they once got from each other. The weight of American

culture has shifted away from universities and toward other information sources. Academics are no longer the gatekeepers of truth.

In response, we see obvious and embarrassing efforts of universities to push themselves into the news. A few years ago the president of my university, a former historian, sent a general memo urging faculty to take this aspect of their job more seriously: "Interacting with the media, producing publications and communicating with our various constituencies and friends is vital to our mission. . . . Florida ranks fifth in academic coverage and third in coverage of athletics. It is important we continue this effort." (He may have missed the fine print, which indicated that the study he referred to included only ten universities.) Up to a point this effort is justified, reminding society of the university's existence, to resist its further decline. But regardless, this points to a symbiosis of news and academics that does not reflect what we used to think universities were about.

The ivory tower is now surrounded by clusters of newspaper vending machines. Not all the papers being dispensed make pretensions to intellectual engagement, of course, and we must wonder how this is serving academic life. I will not be alluding to any bias in the media, whether from liberal editors or conservative publishers. I will not refer to the incompetence of reporters, which we recognize when they report anything within our immediate knowledge. Nor am I lamenting the irresponsibility of celebrity journalists, as profits demand increasing sensationalism. I am not talking about how television dumbs down its product, or the capitalist concentration of the industry, or the techniques of manipulation. These are all things to be concerned about, but they are not the heart of the matter.

My concern is with journalism's dailiness. To imagine that each 24-hour period is worthy of the same attention, or sees the world turn a corner, creates a mindset altogether foreign to science, philosophy, literature, the arts, and religion. Religion is about the eternal as much as about the daily. But the same could be said about other forms of culture. As news infiltrates the thinking of faculty and students, it creates distractions that undermine academic life. Dailiness is a bias all by itself. It governs how the world is presented to us and where the emphasis will lie. I have discussed this at far greater length elsewhere, and will offer only what is relevant to our academic situation here.[1]

1. For more on all this, see C. John Sommerville, *How the News Makes Us Dumb: The*

*   *   *

The only compelling reason for dailiness is that news is now organized as a *business* in our society. If it were a profession, we would call on it as needed, as with doctors and lawyers. But if we waited for something important to happen, we might go weeks without bothering to read news reports. When an issue must be sold each day — or, for that matter, a cable news channel's coverage refreshed every few hours — there is a determination that it be arresting, if not exciting. One of Britain's press magnates, Lord Rothermere, thought that "A newspaper should be like the sea. Every day different and every day the same." Such an enterprise has more pressing concerns than truth, significance, or wisdom.

Be glad that philosophy, say, has not become a periodical enterprise. It would be far livelier if it had to issue its dicta on a regular schedule, but its essential character would be lost. The university should be much closer to philosophy in its organizational implications than to the news.

To think that one can be "informed" about something we call "the world," with its 190 countries and six billion persons, is preposterous. No one thinks that the CIA can do it, and they have 30,000 specialists on the case. Stories about the whole world are what are technically called myths. We may imagine this is what we find in newspapers. There might only be one big story of the day, and we imagine ourselves as informed for knowing it. Being informed turns out to be knowing what others are talking about, so we can take part. Sociologists tell us that this is the real purpose of news, to start the conversations that engender public opinion. Unfortunately we mistake it for something quite different: for information, and even for understanding. Thus we risk losing the disciplines needed for attention to broader views, where truth or wisdom really is the issue.

Even faculties seem to share the view that knowing the day's product from the news industry makes us part of a kind of elite. We may be surprised to find that the truly important people don't rely on the public news. Power could be defined as the ability to keep oneself *out* of the news. Elites could be defined as groups that control certain kinds of in-

---

Death of Wisdom in an Information Society (Downers Grove, Ill.: InterVarsity, 1999), and Sommerville, *The News Revolution in England: Cultural Dynamics of Daily Information* (New York: Oxford University Press, 1996).

formation, which circulates privately. What is left over becomes our daily newspaper. Professors are part of the masses in this regard.

In part, our news addiction may be due to the difficulties of keeping up with our sub-dividing fields of knowledge. We have less and less time to read extensive treatments of the bigger questions, which is still what one expects of university faculties. But we lose a time dimension when we rely mainly on daily reports, which changes our way of looking at society, culture, or science.

Thinking that change is the main thing to think about is perverse. The news does not show us our world, but what has gone wrong with our world. There is a place for that, but it can't be our main outlook on things. Historians reach for a long time horizon in order to judge a thing's significance; it is in the news industry's interest to concentrate on quick change. They find ways of forcing the pace. Partly, this is to destroy the context of each day's reports, to heighten our eagerness for the next edition. To imagine that change is the greater part of reality is an illusion fostered by the bad habit of daily news.

The news cannot help suggesting that truth has a time value. There was a time when the older the wisdom was, the more valuable it was thought to be, the longer it had proved itself. Journalism does not want to be thought captive to past standards. It doesn't have to actually approve the fashions it concentrates on to give the impression that we should move on.

*   *   *

Science, for example, must hardly recognize itself in news reports. Journalists specialize in reporting discoveries that are still in the works. Reporting from the leading edge means offering half-baked reports, preparing us for possible breakthroughs. The implications of these chimeras are likely to be seriously inflated. For it takes a mountain of seemingly insignificant discoveries to establish any general statement — especially a general statement that would make any sense to the general public.

Academic journal articles written by actual scientists would be a serious disappointment to those who are overstimulated by journalistic reports. They would make clear how small the samples are, how correlations are suggestive rather than absolute, how results are indicative rather than conclusive, and how they must always be interpreted.

Though academics might be more sophisticated than others in some respects, when reading outside their own disciplines they are in much the same position as the public.

There is another way in which news reports may distort science. One way for scientists to insure their funding is to send a message through the press. When politicians hear of fascinating proposals, they may pressure funding agencies to adjust their budgets in order to insure a breakthrough. Space programs are especially intriguing to their constituents, and it would be a brave legislator who would stand in the way of exploring the heavens. So science loses control of its enterprise.

Naturally, we are more confident of news reports when they seem to be reporting the thoughts of experts. Yet it is reporters that decide who these experts are. In fact, experts themselves may disagree on who the true experts are. This seems especially important when we hear, as we often do, that the experts disagree. Setting up such conflicts suits the news industry's interests in selling more issues on the subject later, and keeping the pot boiling. Real science is by nature tentative and continuing. But to get our attention, news reports must indicate that the final answer is on the horizon. We would not be as excited if we thought it might be generations before the next scientific plateau was reached.

After all, there is no assurance that science is almost finished, or even halfway there. In the Middle Ages intellectuals were satisfied that they had explanations of everything significant to them. No period has assumed that it lived in darkness. The generation after Newton saw students of science switching out of physics and into biology, convinced that physics was all but complete. We look back pityingly on their naïvete, but Newton himself could not have foreseen the changes of the twentieth century in physics. How can we imagine we are now near a pause?

*   *   *

Where the media's effect on science is probably worst is in reference to the social sciences. Those are the sciences that speak most directly to our condition. Society is a very immediate reality for us, and our social reality changes more quickly than the physical world. Being oriented toward the future, we want to know where changes will be coming from. And while chemists may appreciate being left alone in their labs, social scientists don't mind being featured in the news. Their projects are likely to play to the news industry's current interests.

But social scientists may be just as dismayed as cosmologists at the reporting of their efforts. Every day's news includes poll results, especially those poll items that are controversial or can be politicized. The way they are reported undoubtedly has an effect on cultural attitudes, and perhaps they are intended to. For example, if half of all marriages "work," that is not news — they are supposed to work. If half of all marriages *don't* work, that is news. It is the same situation, of course, but this example shows how our view of society becomes focused on dysfunction and change. If even five percent of all marriages didn't work, those would be the newsworthy ones, since violation, breakdown, conflict, failure — that's news. This conditions our minds away from a necessary scholarly detachment.

So we see here the media's effect in blurring the difference between natural statistical norms on the one hand and cultural values on the other. If statistical norms are changing, involving values we once defended, we may think our culture has no choice but to adjust. We may forget that we have a choice in the values we try to maintain. It is remarkable that our government-sponsored prohibition on mind-bending drugs has remained so uncontroversial, while the incidence of use has become so general. For young readers, especially, may assume that reports of the prevalence of something is tantamount to news approval.

Religion, by contrast, frequently attempts to anchor resistance to what it sees as destructive habits. A secularizing news consciousness may even insinuate that religion's opposition is another reason in favor of the trends. For in the news universe religion often serves as the static foil for something the industry would like to put into play.

In establishing a change of social norms, polling is especially questionable when used as a guide to action or even a window on reality. Pollsters, or the reporters who depend on them, are tempted to force opinion into binary opposition, when reality splits in a dozen ways. The statistics that journalists find so definite must mask wide ranges of opinion and behavior. I have seen headlines declaring that parents and teachers are "split" on some issue, for example, when the fine print indicates that both groups split in roughly equal proportions. A less ambiguous headline would never have caught our attention, and the way articles are written may preserve the confusion. For in reporting about society, it is in the industry's interests to indicate conflict, which justifies further reports. Thus the reporting is a falsification of reality, sharpening conflict and oversimplifying our view. As a result, we may know less than we would from our own observation.

*   *   *

If the sciences are poorly served by a news industry, there is greater damage to other forms of academic culture. For science is not thrown off track to the extent that the rest of our culture may be. Before the birth of a news consciousness, with its demand for dailiness, societies were held together by their cultures, by rough agreement in understandings. Changes were expected to come slowly because new views were supposed to argue down the old ones. After all, culture refers to growth, the word having originally been used of *agri*-culture.

Plants do not thrive when someone keeps pulling them up to check their roots. And we would be surprised if societies could thrive when the cultures that hold them together — more than their economies, governments, or police — are continuously eroded by little more than journalistic suspicion. It is one thing to test our values by substantial and considered scrutiny, as we expect academics to do. It is another thing to relentlessly question the legitimacy of culture, as much by careless allusions as by reasoned engagement. It is in the nature of the news to clear the way for the new.

Universities might be where we address our largest questions in a serious way. But contemporary society seems characterized by the replacement of this dialectic by nothing more substantial than fashion. In a situation of super-specialization, faculty are likely to focus on small-scale questions, so that there is no one in charge of wisdom more generally. In more robust cultures people shared assumptions about the reasonable, the natural, the good. Scholars now use disparaging terms for the things that used to anchor agreement, like master texts, master narratives, myths, and ideologies, and blame them for binding our thought. Cultures fall under the same suspicion. They are seen as that which imprisons our thinking, becoming our second nature. We cannot be entirely free so long as we are unconscious of how culture channels our thinking.

This is true so far as it goes. But what would absolute freedom mean? Must we be endlessly contrary on principle, to keep testing the limits? There is a nihilistic absurdity, not to say insanity, in this effort to attain a total freedom which we could not even define. The structure of a news industry tends toward that, in an endless effort to seek out all that is agreed and put it in play. This is limited only by editors' lack of imagination. News is by definition the new and transgressive, concentrating on violation of norms, values, standards, of all that a culture might build on. The editorial page works against this, by asserting what they see as community values, but this may be as ineffectual as the philosophy page, otherwise known as the comics.

*   *   *

The opposite of all this is the idea of culture, that there are some things that are best settled. Our particular standards of justice, beauty, wisdom, or goodness may be subject to change. They may need continuous attention. But the idea that justice and beauty are very real should not be casually dismissed. Exploring them, rather than playing with the ideas, is what universities were once for.

News cannot replace culture, about which it creates a generalized suspicion. Its job should not be to foster change. It is not of a narrative structure, so it deconstructs itself on a daily basis. Universities are in a position to resist this careless attitude. They might begin by openly questioning the media paradigm which has cast its spell on us.

Sociologists often treat whole societies and cultures as their units of analysis, as if it is the individuals who are the abstractions. This makes a good deal of sense. It is realistic to consider humans as incomplete in themselves, completed by their associations. The way we use cell phones, for example, demonstrates our inability to be alone with our thoughts. Perhaps none of us would survive for a week in a jungle with only ourselves to rely on. Yet our media-driven minds may trick us into thinking of societies as only a convenience by congratulating us on our consumerist independence.

One might question the effect of news discourse on society and culture in terms of respect. Cultures involve respect for their inheritance. Religions should imply respect, probably more than they do. At least it is part of their foundations. Societies and communities must, of course, observe the respect we owe each other as humans and moral ends. But the news naturally fears that it would become lame, lose its edge, by being mostly about respect. Which means that news product should have a limited place in our lives and thoughts. For the fault is not in the industry, which is following its nature, but in us. It is just taking advantage of our addiction.

In these efforts, the university could find an ally in religion. Religions have wrestled with different fundamental principles in a way that news consciousness does not. The individual and community, justice and mercy, tradition and inspiration, the needs of the present and of the future, obedience and creativity, are constant themes within religion as they were in philosophy. News discourse short-circuits debate by the limitations of printing space, broadcast time, or the shortened attention spans it has helped to create. Outside of philosophy departments, our temptations are to be as entertaining as the news succeeds in being. We should know that there is more to learn, but also how to value what others have left us. By attending to religion, universities might help religions build on tradition — while at the same time keeping religion from falling into traditionalism.

Personalist philosophies recognize that we are selves only in relation to other selves.[2] We reach our potential only in the context of our societies. But not, perhaps, in societies whose only unity is found in economic markets, like the market in news. This is why universities have an obligation to enrich their students' understanding and appreciation of their culture. At present, many universities require students to pay attention to other cultures more pointedly than they do their own, which seems curious. When classes encounter elements of their own cultures, the tone is too likely to be ironic. It may be that educators imagine that students have intuited their culture by the time they arrive at university. But there is an increasing question whether they have yet learned anything substantial about it. That might be up to the university.

2. See John Macmurray, *Persons in Relation* (London: Humanities, 1991, orig. 1961).

CHAPTER 14

Spirituality and Decadence

THE CONDITION of our secular universities looks like an instance of the decadence of American society. That is, the universities' lack of assurance, lack of authority, and our lack of interest in their particular enthusiasms are evidence of their having lost an earlier public purpose. We can be happy for what they do accomplish, in training and directing us to our tasks. But it is a melancholy thought that universities might be no help to students who want to use those years to begin building comprehensive worldviews and a sense of what their lives can be about beyond their jobs. It is even worse if those in charge think their job ends with unsettling students' prior convictions and leaving them to pick up the pieces with no real guidance. Is this decadence the natural result of a commitment to the university's secularization?

Of course, we may lament a lack of political engagement, a trashy culture, irresponsible social relations, and a universal ironic disdain, and not connect them to the same sources as the decline of universities. So I must explain what I mean by "decadence." I see a connection between decadence and the now-fashionable use of the word "spirituality." For they seem to point in the same direction.

*   *   *

Decadence is a joke word these days, for use mostly on t-shirts. Does it have a more formal meaning? Obviously it derives from the verb "to decay." What is it to say that something is decaying? To get my students to think about this, I ask them to imagine that they are driving to campus when they happen to hit a squirrel. On their way home they see it beside the road and feel bad, and perhaps reflect on the transitory nature of life. The next day they see it again, and after a week begin to see changes. It's getting flatter, less recognizable, more dried out. Those cells and molecules are losing the relationship they used to have to each other. The squirrel can no longer function as a unit, because it's lost the unifying spark of life. All its elements used to be held together and function together, but now they don't.

Societies can decay in that same way. We've seen societies that are torn apart by violence and revert to more primitive forms of organization. It doesn't always take violence. Societies can lose a sense of common goals, or even of what issues they need to address. They can lose a way to conclude their arguments. They can be held together tenuously by a division of labor, only to find that the labor is not producing anything they want.

The concept of decadence came in handy in my lectures on the history of late medieval England. Historians have puzzled over that period, and why the fifteenth century in England seemed so barren. It almost seems like you could leave the century out and not miss any of those marks of development that one wants students to discover. It was this barrenness, this vacuum, that was filled in the sixteenth century by the Renaissance, the Reformation, the beginnings of the English nation-state. But how was it possible for a period to be so unproductive?

Taking up this question always suggested to students a further discussion about whether the same question can be asked of our time. Are we producing anything of lasting value? Is our art and literature and music just rubbish? Do our institutions really serve the purposes for which they were intended? Or do they only serve selfish interests and actually work against each other? Do our laws work together to create justice, or merely to enrich lawyers? Do our values relate to each other, or do they make a big jumble? Are there core values that hold our culture together, and are they ranked so that we know which ones should override others? What is the level of responsibility among our leaders? What is the level of responsibility among the rest of us?

These are really big questions. Academic historians don't take them up in their professional capacity, because it would seem pretentious. But amateur historians do, because they are the main reason mature people want to study history. We want to know whether the civilization in question serves any higher purpose than enriching a few and keeping the rest from causing trouble. These are the ways we judge the quality of societies. We can't help considering them occasionally, but we don't have the concepts or language that would allow us to think our way through.

Secular universities are uneasy around such questions, because they try to restrict themselves to objective knowledge. They avoid value judgments, about which we may differ. Judgments should only come later. And after more than a century of being officially secular they have forgotten how to apply standards of judgment. It seems rude or silly to try. So they may pretend that such questions are not interesting, or not serious. But they do lurk in the back of everyone's minds.

The very fact that scholars, journalists, and our public intellectuals all avoid large-scale judgments on societies or cultures, or even belittle such considerations, is itself a mark of the decadence of our time. We hesitate to criticize ourselves on such a basic level. Thus we avoid the subject of decadence — or use it facetiously, for some form of naughtiness, like chocolate.

*   *   *

The opposite of "decadence" would be a "cultural synthesis" or an "integral society." All societies used to aspire to something of this sort, and I suppose some came close to achieving it. How could ancient Egypt have survived for thousands of years without tying things together pretty tightly? Some Muslim societies today are making determined efforts in that direction, working to get all their institutions to work together.

We are suspicious of such attempts. There would have to be unifying goals that are not problematic. We in the West have trouble believing that those living in more or less integral societies find them satisfying and don't really crave our often useless freedoms. But the truth is that we have never seriously thought about working toward such goals.

A cultural synthesis would mean that everything in the culture was related to everything else. Art, business, politics, philosophy, schools, families, religious life, all would reflect basic agreement on what is really important in life. It would be the opposite of a chaos of experimental lifestyles. In the Christian Middle Ages, the ultimate end was supposed to be the glorification of God, and secondly, the benefit of others. This embodied the two great commandments in Jesus' teaching, to love the Lord with everything in your being, and your neighbor as yourself.

It was a utopian vision. For example, economics was to be directed toward social ends, not private profit. Naturally the economy would be regulated, since it was for the good of society, and not by an impersonal market or for the profit of a few. The argument that free markets generate more "wealth" than regulated ones might not have impressed them. It is possible to create stacks of money and not have wealth in the sense of well-being. You can see how religion could get involved in this, helping to sort out the ethical questions involved. After all, economics is a main way that we treat our neighbor. How effective is our thinking toward such ends?

Or take art. Art was to glorify God and aid in worship. It wasn't the indulgence of the artist's private vision. This at least had the effect of allowing everyone to participate in the art of the time. It was for public consumption, displayed mostly in churches, and created a common aesthetic language. One didn't have the spectacle of artists lashing out at an unresponsive and unappreciative audience, in ever-more-outrageous statements that died away without a response.

Law was also supposed to be guided by ethical principles. Cheap tricks to manipulate society's rules in one's own interest were recognized as an abuse. The official image of society was as one large organism, a body, in which everyone was a member, like an eye, kidney, or kneecap. If you were no more than a toenail, but were missing or injured, you would be missed and the whole body would suffer and sympathize.

Social classes were considered to be necessary and justified, with each serving a specific purpose, and all contributing to the commonweal. The king was to rule, the nobles to defend, the serfs to work, the monks to pray, the Jews to lend money, and the beggars to offer opportunities for charity. Everyone was accountable, including the pope, who styled himself "the servant of the servants of God." The concept of the "homeless" should not even have arisen.

Of course, anyone who has studied the Christian Middle Ages knows that the period never really achieved the cultural synthesis which beckoned it onward. It would be interesting to see why, rather than to assume that all such efforts are hopeless. This might give us part of the answer to what went wrong in late medieval England. Historians have blamed a breakdown of feudal monarchy and of feudalism itself, which lost an integrating function that had been more realistic at an earlier stage of social development. So the wealth of England was actually increasing in this period, but it was wasted.

Perhaps there was another reason for this decadence. Beyond the decline of feudal loyalties and feudal monarchy, there may have been a sort of exhaustion just as England came closer to achieving that synthesis. There was a lack of imagination at the end, as one can see in the aristocracy's favorite literature, the Arthurian cycle, and the lower orders' favorite literature, Robin Hood. There is a certain aimlessness about both literary cycles, by our way of thinking. Neither one suggests anything like the work ethic that would turn all those classes into productive citizens and that dominates modernity.

In short, it seems that by the end of medieval England individual goals had replaced the community goals of the earlier period, which had been ratified by the church. The church too suffered from institutional ambition and rigidity. So the story of the early Modern period was the dismantling of that effort of cultural and social synthesis. Historians first assumed that this liberation was an unqualified good, and that such a synthesis would violate human freedom. They found it easy to absolutize freedom as a social value. Of course many now have more freedom than they can handle and feel it as a burden. As Daniel Bell has described in the *Cultural Contradictions of Capitalism,* we now face the paradox of balancing our mindless and compulsive production by a mindless and compulsive consumption.

So modern freedom, like money, turned out to be not a value so much as the precondition of all values, the opportunity to find those that one could reasonably give one's life to.

✳   ✳   ✳

Is the university capable of showing a way forward for our decadent society? It is to the university's credit that it does not try to usurp the right of democracy to define our good. But there is little sense that our voting is reaching higher standards as more of our population experiences higher education. In fact, nothing shows our cultural decadence better than how we want to vote on everything. We vote for policies and for politicians of course. But we also vote on American Idol and the Academy Awards. Our newspapers and networks poll us incessantly, in order to maintain the connections between producers and consumers. We are living not just in a political democracy, but in a cultural democracy as well.

It shows weakness when votes take the place of debate, argument, agreement. We settle for voting because we are not practiced at discussing or persuading. Opinion takes the place of reason, and fashion replaces debate. It should be embarrassing that we have so little *in* our heads that we settle for just *counting* them. Polling and voting ought to be the last resort, after exhausting the possibilities of discussion.

The reason discussion of important questions breaks down is that a society and culture lacks that *scale* of values we mentioned earlier. It can't prioritize its goods so that it can see which ones might override others. All values are important, of course, but if you can't rank them you won't be able to have sensible discussions about them. That is where religion comes into the picture. Some overriding value, whatever would top the list, is literally what we mean by religion. When such a thing is ruled out, we have a jumble.

The values that seem least controversial in our entertainment and information media would probably be tolerance and pity. Get on the wrong side of those values and you lose the audience. But what do we do with the more impressive ones, like truth, justice, or charity?

Only one goal can be absolute. The word "absolute" means farthest, ultimate, or transcendent. Actually, theologians have trouble with the notion of absolute *values,* because they think that only God is absolute. There can't be two absolutes — by definition — so if God is absolute all values must be relative to God. You might get away with saying that Christian religion sees love or charity — wanting the best for others — as close to an absolute. But that would have to be qualified by certain understandings of charity, which only become clear in serious discussions. Having God in the equation might keep the debate open, in effect keeping any one expression of charity from being absolutized. Even official secularity is a way of keeping the discussion open, so long as it amounts to neutrality and not a secularist censorship of religious views in principle. That is, so long as it lets religious voices into the conversation.

*　　　*　　　*

Perhaps the most provocative accusation against a decadent culture and society is that it is boring. Fashion is the result of boredom and restlessness. This may be why secularization has produced a context in which fashion is such a dominant factor not just in the clothes we wear, or in our music and entertainment, but in our news product, in our politics, and even in our education. Boredom looks for something to fill up the empty space between birth and death. In the absence of any deadly serious matter like the Cold War, what we have is fashion.

The question has been raised whether decadent societies, or secular ones generally, have the will to survive. Will the reproductive rates in such societies be sufficient to provide a future for them? The main motive for bearing children cannot be to insure that Social Security doesn't go broke. It has been a common criticism of many earlier societies, including ancient Rome, that they simply lacked the population to enable them to continue. And it may be that the secular project of reinventing ourselves may be taking the place of reproducing others.

Fifty years ago, historian Arnold Toynbee used to write about how few of the world's civilizations had managed to generate successful responses to the challenges they faced. Of the twenty-two examples he could identify, only a handful seemed to have a future. His view was that religions rose from the ashes of failed civilizations. They gave birth to the new ones. It seemed to him that the unity and the life principle of societies and cultures were born in some new agreement on ultimate ends. Many have noted that some of the old "world religions" are truly going global these days. Perhaps we are looking at the birth of rejuvenated civilizations.

*   *   *

Recent talk of spirituality comes to mind in this context. Is the current interest in spirituality anything like what Toynbee had in mind? What do you think people intend by saying that they are spiritual but not religious, as so many now do? Some studies of the subject suggest that they want to distance themselves from the more institutionalized aspects of religion. In chapter three I noted the scholarly attempts to find how they were filling the vacuum left by their flight from religion. Spirituality connoted something intrinsic and personally authentic. Other scholars have looked at how the word is being used. One group of researchers reported their findings under the title "Religion and Spirituality: Unfuzzying the Fuzzy." The self-reports they collected most often linked spirituality to "relationship to a Higher Power of some kind," as with religion, but "spiritual" was individual, and more creative.[1] In a book entitled *Spirituality, Diversion and Decadence,* Peter Van Ness represented such people as thinking that "Human existence is spiritual insofar as it intentionally engages reality as a maximally inclusive whole and makes the cosmos an intentional object of thought and feeling," while making one's life "the project of one's most vital and enduring self."[2] As the word becomes more popular, we may reasonably doubt that it always carries that whole freight.

Evidently, "spiritual" means to isolate the *aesthetic* aspect of religion. Aesthetics is about one's sense of things, or awareness of things. The term "aesthetic" was introduced in the nineteenth century to supply *a sense of beauty* with an adjective.[3] So "spiritual" is a way of *looking* at things, and especially at uncanny and arresting things. Religion is about the same experiences, but is *engaged* with these experiences in a way that spirituality is not.

In short, spirituality isn't a way of *doing* things. In religion, one's awareness involves personal demands. Religious persons act on their beliefs about things, or else feel guilty about it. Our definition, you may remember, is that *"religious" is our word for a certain kind of response to a certain kind of power — the kind of response and the kind of power both understood as beyond anything else in our experience.*

The spiritual awareness of something intriguing may remain on the level of the interesting, but it never compels action. Spiritual people may be ethical, but this may have little to do with their spirituality. Spirituality seems to have too little moral weight to be religion. Likewise, spirituality may have too little intellectual content to be philosophy. Like mysticism, it is not an invitation to share insights or join in common projects.

*   *   *

1. Brian J. Zinnbauer, Kenneth I. Pargament, et al., "Religion and Spirituality: Unfuzzying the Fuzzy," *Journal for the Scientific Study of Religion* 36 (1997): 549-64. See also Wade Clark Roof, *A Generation of Seekers* (San Francisco: Harper, 1993), 76f.

2. Peter Van Ness, *Spirituality, Diversion and Decadence* (Albany: State University of New York Press, 1992), 13f.

3. H. W. Fowler, *A Dictionary of Modern English Usage* (London: Oxford University Press, 1944), 12.

Spirituality is apparently what is left of religion in a time of decadence. It does not challenge decadence; it is part of it. Aesthetics recognizes tastes but not imperatives. So while spirituality helps to broaden one's appreciation, it will not be part of a larger cultural project. One cannot speak of the university's need for spirituality, given its intellectual mission.

What a failing society needs, I suspect, is to recover its confidence and its sense of mission. Universities could help by taking a more direct approach to the ethical issues of our time, and not only the popular ones. They need to show that we understand what money is for, rather than being parties to its fetishizing. We need to explore the question of our absolute value.

Of course, religions can become decadent, just as secular societies can. Jesus, for example, had harsh words for those who used religion as a means to dominate others. Churches that are not self-critical will not experience the tension that will keep them alive. And a decadent society will be the worse for it.

In chapter four I argued that instead of the dominance of religious or secular viewpoints, we will benefit from discussion between them. Indeed, most of us have a sort of amphibious relation to both. Instead of culture war, we need a cultural conversation. Instead of secular or religious decadence, we need a tension that would bring greater vitality. Trying to impose one's views works against this kind of balance.

And finally, we must recognize again the damage that results when news product replaces universities as our venue for deciding vital questions. After years of thinking that periodical media make modern societies possible, we need to consider whether news consciousness makes these societies impossible. Are we living in a virtual reality, a society so "overdeveloped" that it can no longer do the things that societies do? Can we socialize children when family patterns are in constant journalistic dispute? Is education shrinking in scope for fear of being publicly stigmatized as traditional? Can we suspend political campaigning between elections long enough to address our pressing problems? Or is the important thing to have our daily referendums on what is happening, since that is what customers will pay for?

Can we manage social debates over the years it may take for our judgment to mature, without trying to personalize the positions? Must they all be forced into dubious dichotomies for the sake of journalistic drama? Could we use the media for the very limited purposes for which they are suited, without imagining that the world fits into their news cycle? We cannot ask the news to change; it is operating according to its nature. Universities used to be thought to have a different nature, and they need to recover that sense.

Religion is functionally the opposite of a news consciousness. We surely need both a journalistic awareness of our moment in time and a sense of timeless realities. They are not in tension or balance today. Secular universities have felt it their duty to screen out religious views because they are controversial. That leaves them more vulnerable to the hegemony of a news consciousness. Yet the bulk of the population also professes some attachment to transcendent views. They have no excuse for not having reasoned views on our issues. If they felt they were in a respectful dialogue with others, it would encourage greater efforts to develop their insights creatively. Such respectful dialogue would also help the most secular minds to do more than simply accommodate all human desires.

Index